THE CHAMPION SPEAKS

"The discerning reader will realize that, by and large, the material of *The Arnold Palmer Method* is not complicated. I have never felt that golf is as complex as some people in the instructional field contend and make it appear. . . . To me, golf is a game that almost any person with a good grasp of a few fundamentals—a sound grip, good body and head position and a smooth, compact swing —can master to such a degree that it will be a constant joy to play."

—from the Introduction,
BY ARNOLD PALMER

D1193767

The Arnold Palmer Method

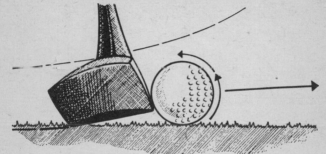

ARNOLD PALMER

A DELL BOOK

CONTENTS

INTRODUCTION *by Arnold Palmer* 7

Chapter 1. THE GRIP 13

Chapter 2. THE STANCE 30

Chapter 3. THE SWING 48

Chapter 4. FROM DRIVING TO CHIPPING 103

Chapter 5. PUTTING 142

Chapter 6. IN AND OUT OF TROUBLE 142

CONCLUSION 235

INTRODUCTION

The son of a golf professional has advantages, I'll admit. My father put a sawed-off golf club in my hands when I was four years old. I grew up at Latrobe Country Club in western Pennsylvania, where my father has worked since the 1920's, and I have had rare opportunites to keep after my game through the years.

It wasn't just that I played a lot, but that I learned the game from the ground up. When I was old enough, I started to caddy and eventually became the caddymaster. Under my father's guidance, I learned just about all there is to know about the structure and construction of golf clubs. The knowledge I acquired about making and repairing clubs has been particularly valuable to me since I formed the Arnold Palmer Golf Company. I have been able to take an active part in the design and analysis of the clubs we sell. My workshop at home in Latrobe is crowded with clubs of all kinds in various states of assembly and disassembly. I thoroughly enjoy working on golf clubs, trying out little changes and refinements that I think might make better clubs. I have even worked on a club or two for other pros on tour and I never leave home for a tournament without knife, tape of various kinds, extra grip and clubs, and my faithful bending iron.

I went right to Wake Forest College from high school, served in the Coast Guard for three years, played amateur golf while working as a salesman, and then joined the pro tour full time. I have never really spent any time to speak of as a "teaching pro" in the usual sense. Oh, occasionally, I'll give a fellow pro or an amateur with whom I'm playing a tip or two about his game, but I have never spent hour after hour on the practice tee with a neophyte golfer.

Actually, I have done a lot of teaching in recent years—by means of the printed page and the airwaves. Probably the biggest "student body" I have reached this way has been a vast group of newspaper readers who have followed and studied the illustrated lessons that have been printed several times a week in newspapers throughout the country for the last five or six years.

Through these tips, I have had the chance to pass along my thoughts and ideas about all phases of the game to golfers everywhere. Because it has been a continuing series, I have had the opportunity to present new material that I have discovered as my experience with the game has grown and, in fact, have on a few occasions revised my thinking on a few techniques through the years.

Unlike the club professional who can watch with pride as a beginner develops into a respectable player under his guidance, I have learned of the help my newspaper lessons have been only when a reader stops me at a tournament or exhibition and tells me about it or writes me a letter. This has occurred often enough for me to feel satisfied that the project is worthwhile.

However, I have long been aware of one uncorrectable weakness of the newspaper series. Unless the reader is a diligent clipper and saver, and practices a great deal in the living room or backyard, the lessons are retained only as long as the memory can hold them. Usually the newspaper goes with the next day's garbage and, for most people, the thoughts slip away rather quickly. From this awareness came the idea for this book—an opportunity to gather together all of the tips since the inception of the series, categorize them, and select the best panels to prepare an illustrated primer of golf instruction, one that will be easy to read and understand as I drive home all the points that any good golf teacher would cover in his instructions on the practice tee.

As you will see, I have broken the subject matter into six chapters, covering virtually all phases of the game. It begins with the fundamentals that any good instructor covers with the beginner or reviews with the golfer who is seeking help for an ailing game—the grip, the stance, and the swing.

With that base, I move into the techniques and tactics involved with the various clubs in the bag, devoting a separate chapter to the all-important phase of putting. Finally, in a sort of catchall chapter, I deal with many of the problems a golfer will encounter on a course—such trouble areas as sand traps and rough; the cures for flaws in the game and the strategies that can keep a player out of trouble in the first place.

The discerning reader will realize that, by and large, the material of *The Arnold Palmer Method* is not complicated. I have never felt that golf is as complex as some people in the instructional field contend and make it appear. Sure, the perfectionist can get mighty technical in explaining the whys and wherefores of the golf swing. But, to me, golf is a game that almost any person with a good grasp of a few fundamentals—a sound grip, good body and head position and a smooth, compact swing—can master to such a degree that it will be a constant joy to play.

I know of few other activities in which people of nearly any age can gain such a feeling of self-satisfaction from a newly acquired skill. There are few things more exhilarating than the pleasure that accompanies that first perfectly struck drive that soars long and straight down the middle of a fairway. Keep in mind, though, that lessons alone will not convert you overnight into a player. Practice is vital. I have always enjoyed practice. Some other touring pros do not, but they still know how important it is. They force themselves to work, work, work on their game.

One final point. I think you can learn much from this book, but there may be times when you will wonder, "What am I doing wrong? Things are not going the way the book says they should."

If this happens, you need a trained golfer to watch you and pick out the flaws in your game. This is where the PGA professional comes in. Don't be too proud to ask for help. It will be well worth the time and money spent.

See you on the course.

—ARNOLD PALMER

The
Arnold Palmer
Method

CHAPTER 1

The Grip

•

When parents correct their children again and again about holding their silverware properly at the dinner table, they aren't concerned solely with etiquette. The natural way a small child grabs a spoon and digs into the food gets the job done, but it certainly does waste a lot of time and motion.

When the beginner takes hold of a golf club, the professional corrects him, too, for pretty much the same reason. Throughout the long history of golf, its practitioners have found only one basic "right way" to grip a golf club and execute a proper golf shot. And this "right way" is not the natural way a person would wrap his hands around the padded, slender metal rod that is the shaft of a golf club. It is a grip that must be pieced together carefully, finger by finger, studied, understood, constantly thought about and practiced until it becomes automatic.

"Wait a minute," somebody is saying. "Aren't there really three different golf grips?" True, in a sense; yet, not true. Actually, there are three variations of the single correct grip, the differences involving the position of a single finger. This you will see in the first illustrations as you proceed through this chapter.

The hands are the golfer's only solid link with the inanimate objects that make up the game—the club and the ball. So, if the hands do not function properly, the club cannot function properly. The hands transmit the player's skill to his weapons.

On the next 15 pages, the reader will find the key lessons I have offered to newspaper readers through the years on the various aspects of the grip—its fundamentals, its importance to the other mechanics of the game, such as the grooved swing and proper balance, and some of the fine points that are a part of the sound grip.

Even if you have been playing the game for some time, it should pay you to study these lessons. Whenever a golfer goes to his club professional for help with his game, the first thing most golf teachers examine for trouble is the grip. This chapter affords the experienced golfer hints for helpful self-diagnosis.

THREE GRIP CHOICES;
TAKE ONE

1

Depending on your hand size and strength, you have three grip choices.

Strong-handed golfers should consider the interlocking grip, in which only three fingers of the left hand rest on the club (see illustration 1).

2

Then there is the "10-finger" grip. Here, both thumbs and all fingers provide a firm hold on the club (see illustration 2).

3

The third grip is my personal choice— the Vardon or overlapping grip (see illustration 3).

The thumb and four fingers of the left hand are placed on the club, and this serves to unify the hands effectively.

IMPORTANCE OF SOUND GRIP

1

In any proper golf grip, your hands should fit snugly together on the club handle and palms should "face" each other (illustration 1).

Such a grip will unify the hands and will help assure a square contact of the club face with the ball.

2

3

Illustration 2 shows a typical slice grip and the grip in illustration 3 will encourage a bad hook. In both, the grip is not "palm-to-palm," as you can see.

The importance of a sound grip becomes apparent when you consider that positioning your hands a fraction of an inch out of proper position on the club will throw your shot off-kilter by 20 or 30 yards.

PROPER GRIP PRESSURE VITAL TO SUCCESSFUL SWING

The pressure you apply in your grip largely determines the success of your swing. Too much pressure tightens your wrists and forearms and restricts their ability to function freely. Too little grip pressure causes the club to slip, usually at the top of your backswing (see illustration 1). Grip slippage not only causes the club face to become misaligned, but also throws your swing out of a proper plane and a good rhythm.

It is impossible to tell you just how firmly you should hold the club. I suggest you grip as lightly as you can and still retain full control of the club throughout the swing.

Illustration 2 shows the fingers that should apply sufficient pressure for club control. These fingers are shaded in the drawing.

A tendency to hook can be minimized by reducing pressure in the right-hand fingers. Increasing grip pressure in these fingers will usually help offset a slice.

ASSUMING A CORRECT GRIP

The process of assuming your grip should become as natural as spooning food into your mouth. You will position your hands correctly on the club if you follow the simple three-step system I show you here.

First, I merely bring my palms together in front of me. Second, I lower my right hand and raise my left.

Notice how this automatically places my right shoulder in proper address position, slightly lower than my left.

Finally, I close my hands around the club shaft.

If you follow this system, your hands will naturally fall into proper gripping position on the club with both palms more or less parallel with the club face.

CONCENTRATE ON THE
LEFT-HAND GRIP

Once the left-hand grip is taken properly, it's simple to get the right hand onto the club correctly. So take more time with the left.

The shaft should cross the left palm diagonally from the bottom (or outer) joint of the forefinger to just below the little finger.

This will produce a so-called strong left-hand grip, in which the "V" formed by the forefinger and thumb points to the right shoulder.

Fold your left hand over the club and see that the thumb rests slightly to the right-top part of the shaft.

PROPER POSITIONING OF RIGHT HAND

1

In illustration 1 we see a common grip fault that can only lead to inconsistent shot-making. The golfer has gripped the club too much in the palm of his right hand, much as a baseball player would hold the bat.

2

In a proper grip the club should pass across the top of all four fingers of the right hand (illustration 2). It shouldn't lay against the palm.

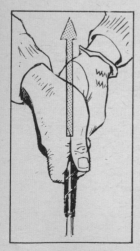

3

When the right hand is closed around the club (illustration 3), the "V" between the right thumb and forefinger should point approximately at your chin.

In other words, the right hand grips the club almost entirely in the fingers. Such a grip gives you maximum "feel" and control of the club. It also places the right palm in a position that more or less parallels the face of the club. This enables you to return the club face squarely to the ball time after time.

HELPING YOUR SHOT TO RISE

Because the left hand is most susceptible to loosening during the swing—especially at the top of the backswing—special care must be taken to see that this hand affords firm club control.

To check if your left-hand grip is firm, place the club alongside this hand (see illustration 1). Close the hand, as in illustration 2. Then raise the club to eye level and open the last three fingers (illustration 3).

If your club is properly positioned, against the fleshy pad below your little finger, it will support itself against this pad and in the crooked forefinger when you open the fingers. If you cannot support the club this way, go back to the first step and recheck the proper relationship between hand and club.

POSITION POINTERS FOR LEFT HAND

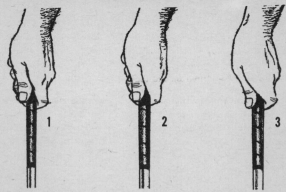

The position of the club face during the swing is largely dominated by the left hand. Thus, taking the grip with this hand is especially important.

If you tend to hit the ball with a closed club face, grip so that your left hand is turned more to your left at address (see illustration 1).

In illustration 3, you'll notice that the hand is turned well to the player's right on the club. If the left hand is in the same position at impact, he'll get a straight shot. I recommend this grip for all chronic slicers.

If, however, this hand is turned more to his left at impact than it was at address, the club face will be closed and a hook will result (see illustration 2).

KEEP WRISTS HIGH AND READY
FOR ACTION

Does your wrist positioning resemble that shown in illustration 1? Congratulations, low handicapper. You're learning fast. The wrists at address should be high, alert, ready for action. No sag (as in illustration 2), no wrinkles visible on the tops of the wrists.

The major function of any full swing is to return the club face squarely to the ball—to return it to the same position it was in at address. Conversely, a player's address position should closely approximate the position he will be in at impact. As the wrists must be high at impact, it is better if they are high at address.

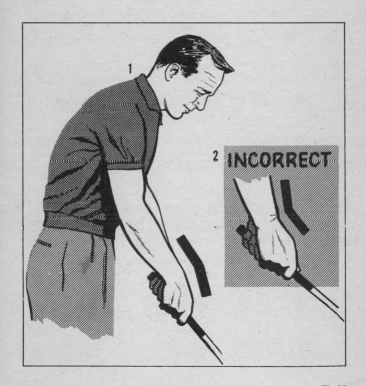

PROPER RIGHT-HAND PRESSURE
PROMOTES "LATE HIT"

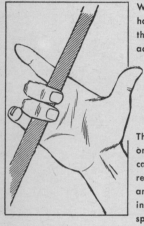

When the two middle fingers of the right hand grip the club firmly, the muscles on the inside of the right forearm—at the address position—tighten.

This localized grip pressure is important on the downswing (see illustration) because it makes the golfer more likely to return his right elbow to his right side, an action that produces a "late" uncocking of the wrists and maximum club-head speed.

Golfers who put too much grip pressure on their right thumb and forefinger tense the muscles on the outside of their right forearm. This may cause the right elbow to float on the downswing and the wrists to uncock prematurely.

I don't advise excessive grip pressure in these two middle fingers. That might cause you to loosen your grip with the other fingers. Just make sure your grip with the middle fingers of your right hand is especially firm.

A FIRM LEFT HAND IS ESSENTIAL

In this illustration, the player's left hand has come completely off the shaft. This can ruin your control over the club. Often the club handle will shift in the grip, and there's no telling where the club face will be pointed at impact. This also will allow the right hand to take over at this point, causing a "cast" or early wrist uncocking too soon in the downswing.

Here the left-hand grip is firm; the situation is under control.

The butt end of the handle should fit in snugly against the fat part of the left hand, and below the little finger, as shown. Now the golfer can start the club head back down to the ball smoothly and slowly. His wrists will remain cocked until the moment before impact when he needs the wrists' whiplash power.

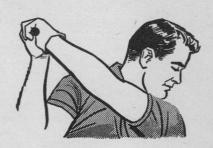

PLAYING UNDER PRESSURE

There is a normal tendency, when playing under unusual pressure, to increase the firmness of your grip. This is bad because a grip that is too firm encourages a jerky swing, and a jerky, hurried swing is especially harmful in tight situations when you need the best, smoothest swing you can muster.

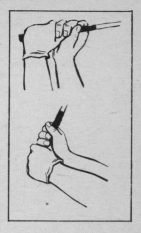

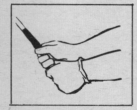

When you feel pressure, be it on the tee or on the green, relax your grip. Don't get sloppy about it; just relax a little in your hands.

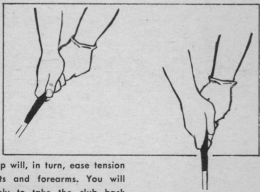

A relaxed grip will, in turn, ease tension in your wrists and forearms. You will be more likely to take the club back smoothly and put yourself in position for a smooth, unhurried downswing.

KEEP SWING "IN THE GROOVE"

1

Take a look at the correct, effective grip shown in illustration 1. It is one that is guaranteed to keep your swing on a normal plane.

2

The grip in illustration 2 is too "strong." With both hands turned too far to the right, your swing plane will be too flat and, on iron shots, you won't be able to swing downward properly and contact the ball before the turf.

3

A "weak" grip (illustration 3) tends to produce an upright swing plane, which can cause topped shots. Such a grip also can cause an outside-in swing which, in turn, gives you a slice—when you don't want one.

PROPER GRIP PRODUCES BALANCED SWING

It is truly amazing how greatly an almost imperceptible change in a golfer's grip can alter his swing. I find that when I grip with my hands turned too far to my right (see illustration 1), I have a tendency to sway my body laterally to the right on my backswing. If my hands are turned too far to the left (see illustration 2), I seem to want to raise my body on the backswing. Obviously, swaying and raising the body during the backswing will destroy a player's sense of balance.

1

2

3

To grip the club in a manner that will encourage a balanced swing, I imagine that the club face is merely an extension of my right palm (illustration 3). Both the palm and the club face are looking at the target. When they are aligned in this manner, my hands will be in a position to provide a balanced stroke.

CHECK YOUR GRIP PERIODICALLY

Check your grip periodically to see that (1) the club handle rests on the third joint of the index, middle and third fingers of the right hand; (2) the left hand is firmly in place, with no space showing around the hand at the butt end of the club; (3) the right forefinger is "cocked" a bit down the shaft.

Here's the standard grip from another perspective. Note that the right thumb is stationed a bit on the left-top side of the club.

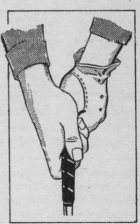

For most golfers, the V's formed by the thumb and forefinger of both hands point toward the right shoulder. As you look down at your grip, you should see only one knuckle of the right hand, two of the left.

CHAPTER 2

The Stance

●

Next in logical succession in preparing a newcomer to play golf is the stance. The word "stance" covers more than just the positioning of the feet. The professionals usually talk about "setting up to the ball," a phrase that encompasses several factors that a golfer must consider before he is ready to take his swing at the ball.

In the discussion of the grip, it was pointed out that the proper way to hold a club is not the natural way. Until the player gets used to it, the golf grip does not feel necessarily comfortable. In standing up to a shot, though, comfort is the big thing.

As the lessons and illustrations in this chapter show, the golfer stands neither stiffly erect nor crouched far forward, reaching for the ball. Instead, he stands in a slight crouch, knees slightly flexed, the arms hanging normally down from that position.

Alignment with the target of all parts of the body is another important aspect of stance, or setting up to the ball. Talking about the driver (because the stance tends to open as the player gets to the shorter irons), it is stressed that, not just the feet, but also the hips and shoulders must be parallel with the imaginary line from player to target.

The position of the ball in relation to the feet and

the distance between the two feet are other important considerations for the player before each shot. These will vary both from player to player and, of course, with each player himself, depending on the club he has in his hands.

My lessons deal with these variations for the average player, offering, for instance, the general rule of thumb that the width of the stance should approximate the width of the golfer's shoulders. Don't be misled because you have seen a few of the touring pros who use a noticeably wider or narrower stance. Similar exceptions hold true for the positioning of the ball in relation to the stance, as there are times when, to execute properly a particular, out-of-the-ordinary shot, the ball must be played farther forward or back in the stance than would normally be the case.

Although it is discussed more extensively in relation to the swing, the positioning of the head is of great importance at address. Once it is in position over and just slightly behind the ball, it must stay there until the golfer is well into his follow-through. In other words, the feet and head are anchored at address and the swing revolves around this axis.

One final, important point contained in this chapter balance through proper weight distribution. The golfer must have good balance before he starts the swing.

POSITION OF FEET DETERMINES DIRECTION OF SHOT

The stance a golfer employs largely determines the direction in which his shots will fly. There are three stances in golf—square, closed and open.

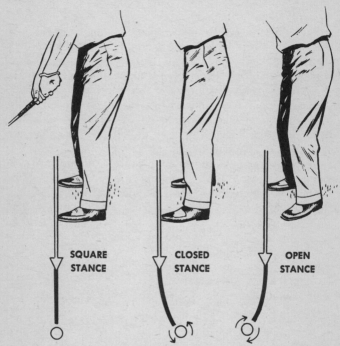

SQUARE STANCE   CLOSED STANCE   OPEN STANCE

All things being equal, the square stance will produce a straight shot. The club head will be moving along the line to the target when it strikes the ball. Thus, the ball will fly with perfect backspin—no side-spin that would make it fly left or right.

From a closed stance, however, the club head will be moving from inside to outside the target line during impact. This will impart a right-to-left spin that will make the ball hook to the left.

The open stance will cause the club head to move to the ball from outside to inside the target line. A left-to-right spin results, causing the ball to slice to the right.

SPREAD YOUR FEET SHOULDER WIDTH AT ADDRESS

Many golfers could improve their shot-making immeasurably by increasing or decreasing the width of their stance.

In a proper stance your feet should be spread far enough apart to provide a firm foundation for your swing. However, a stance that is too wide will restrict leg action and body turn.

Everyone has to find his own proper stance width. I personally like to feel that the distance between my inner soles equals the spread between the outer edges of my shoulders (see illustration). I think this might be a good guide for most players.

However, if you seem to have trouble making a full turn, try a narrower stance. If you have trouble maintaining balance during your swing, try a wider stance.

SQUARE YOUR HIPS AND SHOULDERS

All things being equal, the average golfer should be "square" when he addresses the ball. He should position himself so that imaginary lines across his toes, hips and shoulders are parallel to an imaginary line from the ball to the target. If a golfer is so positioned, his club head should move along that target line at impact and long, straight shots should result.

Many golfers make the mistake I am demonstrating in illustration 1. Note that my feet are parallel to the target line, but that my hips and shoulders are turned a bit to my left so that they slightly "face" the target. This position encourages slicing.

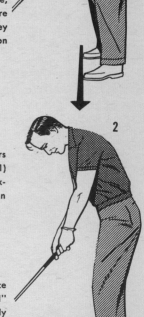

To make sure your hips and shoulders are also square, imagine two lines: (1) a line to the target and (2) a line extending at right angles (dotted line in illustration 2) to the target line.

When you address the ball, merely place your body so it looks down this "dotted" line. In so doing, you will automatically position your hips and shoulders "square" to the target line.

ONLY A SLIGHT BEND FOR SOLID CONTACT

1

The crouched position at address (illustration 1) encourages a lifting of the body and head and a straightening of the knees during the swing. Naturally, this produces mis-hit shots.

2

At address, stand with your knees only slightly bent and your arms hanging straight with no bend at the elbows (illustration 2). The left arm especially should be extended. This will give you, overall, a more upright address position. Your body will be in more or less the same position at address that it will assume at impact.

HANDS AHEAD—AT ADDRESS AND IMPACT

As I have often stressed in the past, a golfer can expect good shot results if his hands are positioned at address in approximately the same position they will be in when his club head strikes the ball. Obviously, if a golfer positions his hands behind the ball at address (illustration 1) and then leads with his hands at impact (illustration 2), some compensation must be made during his swing.

I think it's much better to address the ball as I am in illustration 3. Note that the hands are slightly forward of the club head. The left arm and club shaft more or less form a straight line, just as they should during impact.

It was only recently that I personally positioned my hands forward at address in the manner I now advocate. I find that this new address position has made it easier for me to execute a unified one-piece swing.

ADDRESS POINTERS

At address, always pay close attention to the "lie," that is, the angle formed by the club's shaft and head. Illustration 1 shows what I mean.

If the toe of the club is raised (as in B), you'll wind up with a hook. If the heel is raised (as in C), a slice can result. Better to have the sole of your club lie flat on the ground (A).

If you're short and must stand farther from the ball, make use of a flat swing and clubs with relatively flat lies. Tall golfers, or others with an upright swing (illustration 2), usually stand closer to the ball and thus require an upright lie on their clubs.

LINE UP SQUARE

Because some golfers don't understand the construction of golf clubs, they line up incorrectly.

If you use the top edge of the club head, especially an iron, with which to line up your shot, you'll probably be in a closed position. The top edge of most modern iron club heads flares out.

See how this golfer has lined up—his shot will likely fly left.

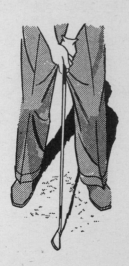

A proper lineup uses the bottom edge of the club head as the focal point. When it's lined up square to the intended line, the upper edge will flare a bit to the rear of the golfer—a direction away from the target.

Here the club head is lined up correctly. Bring it back to the ball in this position and your chances of a good shot will improve.

"BOW" YOUR RIGHT SIDE

Obviously, the golfer's attention should be on the back of the ball. Yet, many golfers make this difficult by placing too much weight on their left foot at address. Such weight distribution also encourages premature cocking of the wrists on the backswing and, hence, a narrow swing arc.

To assure a proper weight distribution, to enable my attention to focus on the back of the ball, and to more or less "preview" my impact position, I prefer to "bow" my right side slightly at address.

To be more specific, this bow is achieved by bending my hips slightly toward the target and my right knee a bit toward the ball. The longer the shot, the more pronounced the bow.

You will readily note that this positioning sort of duplicates how it should be when you come into the ball.

Just make sure your hips do not turn to the left when you assume this position. "Opening" the hips in this manner encourages slicing.

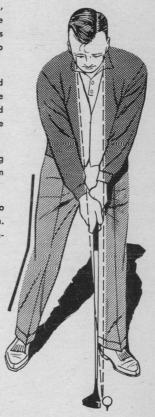

DETERMINING BALL POSITION

The shorter the club you use, the more forward should be your stance. The position of the club face, or hitting area, changes in relation to the shaft for each club. The driver club face is bulged well ahead of the shaft, but the wedge's hitting area is actually behind (in relation to the target) a line drawn straight down the shaft. A player, positioning the ball in the same spot for a wedge as for a drive, would have to move his body forward (toward the target) to achieve the same impact. Play the drive off the left instep, then move forward on down the line to a 5-iron, halfway between the instep and stance center, and finally to the wedge, which should be near stance center for a normal shot.

ANGLING IN THE RIGHT KNEE

It is very important for proper balance that golfers keep their weight centered during the swing.

You should feel downward pressure on the insides of your feet as you address the ball. I have shown this in illustration 1. You will also note in this illustration that my right knee is angled slightly inward. This knee position forces me to keep my weight properly on the inside of my right foot.

During my backswing in illustration 2, you can see that this right knee no longer bends inward, but my weight still remains on the inside of the foot.

On the downswing (illustration 3), inward pressure becomes even greater as I "push off" on the instep, and the right knee again angles toward the target.

HIP POSITIONING HAS GREAT EFFECT ON SHOT DIRECTION

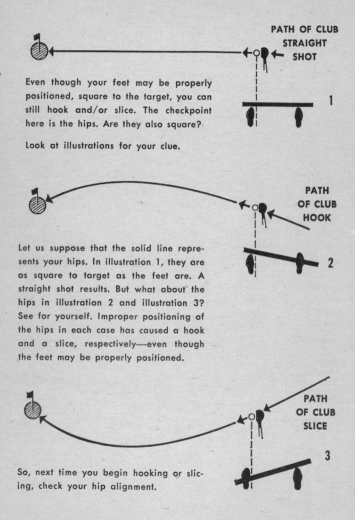

PATH OF CLUB STRAIGHT SHOT

1

Even though your feet may be properly positioned, square to the target, you can still hook and/or slice. The checkpoint here is the hips. Are they also square?

Look at illustrations for your clue.

PATH OF CLUB HOOK

2

Let us suppose that the solid line represents your hips. In illustration 1, they are as square to target as the feet are. A straight shot results. But what about the hips in illustration 2 and illustration 3? See for yourself. Improper positioning of the hips in each case has caused a hook and a slice, respectively—even though the feet may be properly positioned.

PATH OF CLUB SLICE

3

So, next time you begin hooking or slicing, check your hip alignment.

SETTING UP TO THE BALL

1 Sooner or later golf must become a habit if you want to succeed. As you become proficient, you find yourself doing the same thing the same way time after time.

One area in which it is especially important to have a set pattern is in setting up to the ball.

I have a 3-step pattern that brings me up to the point where I'm ready to start waggling the club. First, I size up the shot from behind and to the side of the ball, as you see me doing in illustration 1. At this time I check the best line to the target and consider the proposed flight of the ball. Next (illustration 2), I place the club head squarely behind the ball so that the club face looks down the target line. Finally, I assume my stance (illustration 3).

2

3

It is important that step 3 not precede step 2. If you take your stance before aligning the club face, you might force yourself to "reach" for, or "crowd," the ball.

PLAN STANCE WHILE APPROACHING BALL

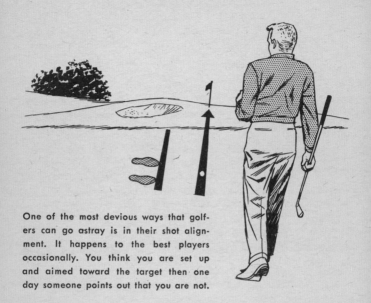

One of the most devious ways that golfers can go astray is in their shot alignment. It happens to the best players occasionally. You think you are set up and aimed toward the target then one day someone points out that you are not.

One way to check your alignment is to visualize a line from the ball to the target as you walk up to the ball (see illustration). Also visualize a line that parallels the target line. This is the line that should run across your toes.

Then, when you address the ball, put your toes up to this second line.

This will automatically give you a square stance. If you place your club face behind the ball at right angles to the target line, it will be facing in the direction you wish your shot to take.

STAY IN CONTINUOUS MOTION

Set up a pre-shot procedure to follow each time. This will help defeat nervous tension.

I always walk up to the ball from behind, survey the situation and then select a club. It's easier to get a line on the angle of the shot from behind the ball.

Once the club is selected, I assume a position just short of my final stance. My feet will be closer together than they will be when I get ready to swing, but my grip will be in place.

I like to look down the fairway and picture my shot flight.

Although I don't take a practice swing, some golfers do and feel it helps. Of course, before I swing, I waggle the club head by moving it over the ball. This is all part of my system not to let my muscles tense up.

CHECK THAT STANCE

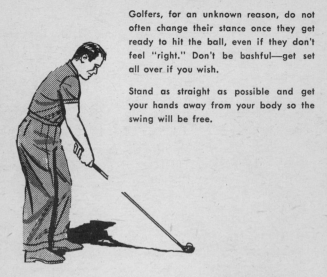

Golfers, for an unknown reason, do not often change their stance once they get ready to hit the ball, even if they don't feel "right." Don't be bashful—get set all over if you wish.

Stand as straight as possible and get your hands away from your body so the swing will be free.

You'll know if you were set right once the backswing starts. If you can turn at the hips easily, keeping the club head low to the ground and the wrists unbroken as you start back, your golf shot is likely to be good.

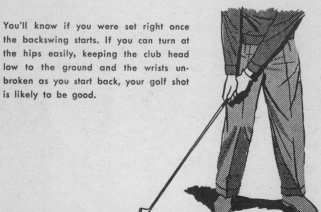

STANCE ADJUSTMENT CAN CURE SWING PROBLEMS

Your stance directly affects your swing. It follows, therefore, than an adjustment of your stance can eliminate certain swing faults.

In illustration 1 we see the typical "square" stance. A line across the toes runs parallel with a line from the ball to the target.

In illustration 2 we have the "open" stance with the forward foot pulled back from the line. Such a stance will help golfers who have trouble clearing their left hip and side on the downswing. This stance also restricts the backswing and, thus, would help golfers who tend to overswing going back.

The "closed" stance in illustration 3 will help golfers complete a fuller backswing turn, but might restrict the follow-through. Such a stance should help players who have a tendency to slice.

CHAPTER 3

The Swing

•

The preliminaries are over. Now it's action—the swing of the club and the flight of the ball.

The successful swing must be executed in one flowing motion, but for discussion and instructional purposes it can be broken up into five distinct phases—the takeaway, the completion of the backswing, the downswing, contact with the ball, and the follow-through. If procedure is incorrect in any of these components of the swing, smooth, compact action cannot be achieved.

On the takeaway, for instance, I stress how important it is that all parts of the body involved in the backswing move together, emphasizing that the wrists must not break too soon, a common fault of novice golfers.

How far back do you go? This chapter points out that the length of the backswing varies with the individual and the club being used. It also cites the danger of over- and underswinging.

The wrist break is again stressed in the discussions of the downswing. It can't be said too often that the golfer expends his power and disrupts the proper swing arc when he uncocks his wrists too early in the downswing.

All instruction thus far has been designed to get the club face onto the ball correctly in the impact zone —the goal the leading professionals reach virtually all of the time, the goal the average golfer will reach probably only often enough to keep him coming back for more, searching for the elusive groove that will reduce his handicap. The cardinal point made about the impact zone is that the greater the distance the club face travels to the ball in the correct square position, the longer and more accurate the resulting shot will be.

Perhaps the thing that confuses the new golfer most is the talk about the importance of the follow-through. The ball is already on its way, he reasons. How can the follow-through possibly affect the shot? It doesn't, really, but it is the indicator of the type of swing you have made. It is virtually impossible to have an abbreviated or flat follow-through at the end of a good swing. The poor follow-through is the warning signal that something has gone wrong earlier in the swing.

One phase of the swing that is given scant attention is the method of starting the downswing. This has been de-emphasized on purpose, because I feel that the weight shift back to the left side and its accompanying motions come naturally, and that conscious thoughts about shoulder, hip, knee, and left hand pulling down toward the ball clutter up the player's mind and consequently the smoothness of his swing. A steady head and good balance on firmly planted feet are the important factors.

WAGGLE WITH A PURPOSE

Before starting your backswing, free your wrists and hands from tension by waggling the club head.

The waggle also serves another purpose. It sets the pattern of your takeaway. The movement of your club head during your waggle more or less previews the path your club head will take at the start of your backswing.

Therefore, I feel it is unwise to raise and lower your club head (see illustration 1) during your waggle. Such movement might cause you to lift your club head abruptly on your takeaway.

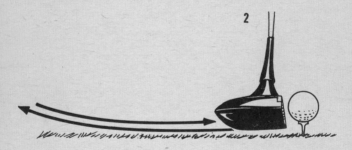

Instead waggle by moving the club head backward and forward behind the ball, more or less in the same groove it will assume during your swing (illustration 2). Your takeaway should find the club head moving straight back from the ball and low to the ground. Your waggle should follow this same pattern.

FORWARD PRESS OVERCOMES INERTIA

If golfing physics professors practice what they teach, they are probably unanimous in their use of the forward press.

The forward press helps overcome inertia, the tendency of an object at rest to remain at rest. The golf swing should be a continuous movement and it's the forward press that starts this movement.

In a normal forward press, the hands and right knee should move just slightly toward the target (illustration 2).

Though the forward press is a move toward the target, it really should be considered part of the backswing. It does precede the takeaway, but there should be no noticeable halting of motion between the two. Press forward and then move continuously into the backswing (illustration 3).

START SWING WITH WRISTS FIRM

There should be nothing sloppy about your golf swing, especially during the early stages of the backswing. Illustrations 1 and 2 show improper takeaways, with the player's wrists hinging prematurely. The results of such sloppy takeaways include a narrow swing arc, which minimizes distance, and an improperly aligned club face at impact, which decreases not only distance but also accuracy.

The wrists should remain firm, not stiff, during the takeaway. The golfer should feel that the club shaft is a direct continuation of his left arm until the hands are hip-high (as I show in illustration 3). The club head should move back and up as a result of the player's tilting and turning of his body and shoulders, not as a result of any independent hinging of the wrists. The wrists should hinge automatically later in the backswing.

This firm-wristed takeaway will give you a wide swing arc and full coiling of your muscles. It will also keep the club face in a proper position to return squarely to the ball without any independent manipulation of the hands on the downswing.

This is one way to keep your swing simple, to derive maximum distance and accuracy.

HERE'S PROPER TAKEAWAY

The first few inches of the backswing takeaway can determine how effective or ineffective your shot will be.

1

Thus, from the normal address position, many golfers start backswinging with only their hands, leaving the club head at the ball (see illustration 1). You can see how this closes the club face and cuts down on accuracy.

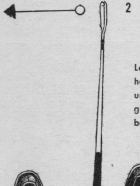

2

Let your takeaway involve the arms, hands and club, moving together as a unit (see illustration 2), as your body begins its normal turn to the right in the backswing.

START RIGHT SHOULDER LOW

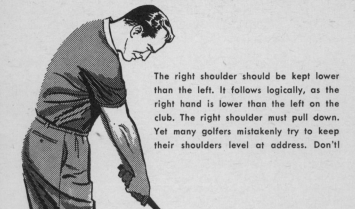

The right shoulder should be kept lower than the left. It follows logically, as the right hand is lower than the left on the club. The right shoulder must pull down. Yet many golfers mistakenly try to keep their shoulders level at address. Don'tl

Once you start out right with this slanted shoulder position, your body is set for a compact swing. Nearing impact, the right shoulder returns to this original low position, and you'll find it easier to keep the right elbow tucked into the side, as illustrated. This encourages a good swing, slightly from inside the intended line of flight, and square contact with the ball.

WRIST COCK VARIES WITH THE SHOT

Normally, I would not advise golfers to be concerned about when their wrists begin to cock on the backswing. The wrists should cock automatically when the hands reach about hip height.

However, it is important to note that the wrists do cock earlier on short shots than on shots with the woods and long irons. You will note in the illustrations that, though the hands are about at a similar height, the wrist cock is much more noticeable on the short iron shot.

On long shots there is more emphasis on distance. Therefore you need a wider swing arc. The hands and arms should push the club away from the body on the backswing, even if the right elbow must move away from the right side. All this results in a later cocking of the wrists.

On short shots, where the premium is on accuracy, you want a more compact swing. The right elbow should remain close to your side. This forces a more upright backswing and an earlier cocking of the wrists.

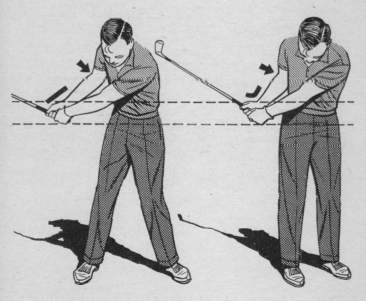

WIDE BACKSWING ARC INCREASES POWER

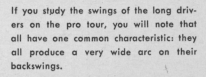

If you study the swings of the long drivers on the pro tour, you will note that all have one common characteristic: they all produce a very wide arc on their backswings.

A wide swing arc produces a longer club-head path than does a narrow swing arc. Normally, a long club-head path produces more club-head speed at impact, and thus more distance. A wide swing arc, if properly produced, also encourages a full shoulder turn, another major source of power.

I produce a wide backswing arc by maintaining a fully extended left arm throughout. Also, I take the club head straight back from the ball.

It is very important, however, that your head and your body do not sway laterally to the right on your backswing. This is a normal tendency when one strives for a wide swing arc. Swaying will destroy all benefits derived from the wide swing arc. So swing the club head straight back, then around and up, with a straight left arm—but don't sway to the right.

ACHIEVE THE TIGHT ELBOW POSITION

Note in the illustrations how my right elbow barely leaves my right side.

Most golfers can achieve a tight right elbow position on their backswing by increasing the degree of their shoulder turn. The more the shoulder turn moves the hands back and up, the less the hands and arms will have to raise on their own to achieve a backswing of sufficient length and height.

Concentrate on making a full shoulder turn and keeping your right elbow in fairly close to your side. You will find that this not only makes your swing more compact, but also provides you with a full coiling of muscles for greater distance on shots.

EXCESSIVE HEEL LIFT LESSENS POWER AND DISTANCE

1

Compare the two heel lifts in illustrations 1 and 2.

One, you can see, is excessively high, while the other is correctly moderate.

2

The player in illustration 1 is curtailing both power and distance. Such a "toe dance" will keep him from coiling the muscles of the left side of the body on the backswing. On the downswing, therefore, when these muscles should uncoil, his club-head force won't have much oomph.

So keep the heel lift moderate. The muscles will then have a better chance to coil on the backswing and uncoil on the downswing—for more power and force.

BACKSWING AND SWAY

If you are suffering from directional errors as well as a loss of distance, it may be because you are swaying on the backswing.

The player in illustration 1 is swaying because he is moving his body laterally to the right instead of tilting and turning his shoulders and torso on a central axis. The other golfer (illustration 2) is "coiling" his body correctly.

If you make certain that your weight remains primarily on the inside of your right foot (illustration 3), without moving to the outside, your chances of eliminating sway are good.

HOW TO GROOVE THE BACKSWING

If your swing is too flat, or too upright, let a friend watch you in action. Your left arm should cross your right shoulder (as seen by your friend watching from behind you, on the intended line of flight).

A player may allow himself slight variances, according to his build and other factors. But any crossing far away from this point is undesirable.

If a golfer's left arm crosses the shoulder well below the tip (illustrated), his swing is much too flat. He will probably be subjected to duck hooks, when and if he does manage to contact the ball square.

A too upright swing will find the left arm crossing the shoulder well up into and near the neck. Often this causes a "flying" right elbow, making the club head more difficult to control.

DON'T COPY MY BACKSWING

My backswing works fine for me, but I take the club back too fast for most average golfers' swings.

A too-fast backswing will wreck your timing because it doesn't allow you to sense the position of your hands or the feel of the club head. Also, you can lose balance when you begin the downswing after a speedy backswing.

Remember, the whole purpose of the backswing is to set yourself up for a strong downswing. It also lends rhythm to the entire swing.

So, if you feel your swing is off somehow, try slowing down the backswing. Your timing, direction and balance can improve plenty.

BACKSWING SPEED DEPENDS ON PLAYER'S TEMPERAMENT

Backswing speed is, in my opinion, up to you as long as you can make a full turn, retain a firm grip on the club and keep in balance.

If the backswing is too fast, you may expend too much energy and not have enough for the downswing. If the fast backswing stems from anxiety to hit the ball, it may produce a premature unhinging of the wrists on the downswing. Also, fast backswings tend to be short and you fail to stretch fully your muscles.

If your backswing seems too short, if you loosen your grip at the top, or if you have a problem maintaining balance, I'd suggest you try a slower backswing.

A BACKSWING CHECKPOINT

More often than not, the basic fault in a golfer's swing—the one error that produces other troubles—occurs before the hands have moved higher than the hips on the backswing.

A common error that produces inconsistency is the tendency to open or close the club face—rather than to keep it square—on the backswing. Here is a simple way to check the position of your club head on the backswing:

When your hands are as high as your hips on the backswing, note the direction that the back of your left wrist is facing. It should be facing forward, as in illustration 1.

If it is facing upward, you have rolled your club face into an open position (illustration 2). If it looks down toward the ground, you have a closed club face (illustration 3).

Always try to swing into the first position. This will give you a square club face that will probably return squarely to the ball.

SHOULDERS HELP DETERMINE DIRECTION

The way a golfer turns his shoulders on the backswing does much to determine whether or not his shot will fly fairly straight.

If the shoulders have tilted and turned properly on the backswing so that the left shoulder has lowered and moved under the player's chin, the club should be pointing along the target line at the top of the swing, as in illustration 1. From this position, the player has an excellent chance of returning the club face squarely to the ball along a path that will insure a reasonably straight shot.

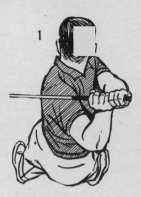

In illustrations 2 and 3, I show you the results of an incomplete and an excessive shoulder turn respectively. It is possible to hook, slice, push or pull the shot from either of these positions, depending on the return path of the club head.

I suggest that, if you hook or slice, have a friend or professional check the alignment of your club shaft at the top of your swing. If it varies a good deal from pointing along the target line, you should see about correcting your shoulder turn.

POINT LEFT SHOULDER AT THE BALL

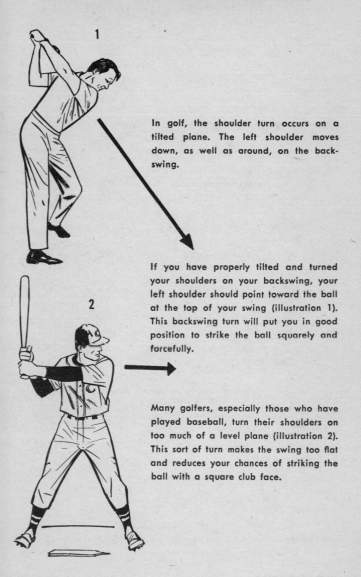

In golf, the shoulder turn occurs on a tilted plane. The left shoulder moves down, as well as around, on the backswing.

If you have properly tilted and turned your shoulders on your backswing, your left shoulder should point toward the ball at the top of your swing (illustration 1). This backswing turn will put you in good position to strike the ball squarely and forcefully.

Many golfers, especially those who have played baseball, turn their shoulders on too much of a level plane (illustration 2). This sort of turn makes the swing too flat and reduces your chances of striking the ball with a square club face.

WHAT CONSTITUTES OPEN, CLOSED AND SQUARE CLUB FACES?

Open, closed and square club-face positions apply to the direction in which the club face points at the top of the backswing.

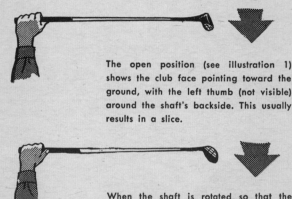

The open position (see illustration 1) shows the club face pointing toward the ground, with the left thumb (not visible) around the shaft's backside. This usually results in a slice.

When the shaft is rotated so that the club face points in any direction upward (see illustration 2), the position is closed. This position may reduce slicing but may cause a pull to the left.

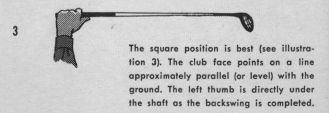

The square position is best (see illustration 3). The club face points on a line approximately parallel (or level) with the ground. The left thumb is directly under the shaft as the backswing is completed.

HOW FAR TO SWING BACK

1

Length of backswing does not have as much effect on shot distance as many believe. There are many other, more important factors. If you don't believe this, look at the relatively short backswing of Jack Nicklaus (illustration 1), possibly the longest driver of all time. I take my driver back to about a horizontal position on the backswing (illustration 2).

You should swing back just as far as you can without losing control of the club in your hand, as has happened in illustration 3. A controlled backswing is much preferred to a long but loose backswing. I'd rather see golfers swing a bit on the short side than to have them strain for a long backswing. Remember that "control" is the key word when talking about backswings.

2

3

SHORTER BACKSWING WITH IRON, LONGER WITH WOOD

You would think it obvious that on tee shots you should make a much fuller body and shoulder turn than on shorter approach shots. After all, you are using a longer club off the tee, and you are striving for more distance.

Yet, many golfers take too little of a turn on tee shots and too much of one on approach shots with the middle and short irons.

Always make sure to take a full turn on tee shots. Stretch those back and shoulder muscles on your backswing so you get a full release of power coming down. Failure to take a full turn on wood shots often causes slicing.

Then, on approach shots, where the accent is on accuracy rather than distance, take a shorter swing with less body turn. A long swing with a short club can only undermine accurate approaching.

Study the illustration, showing a shorter swing with the iron and a longer swing with the wood. Then recall this picture the next time you play.

CLUB "ON TARGET" AT START OF DOWNSWING

The direction your club is pointing just before you start your downswing largely determines the direction your shot will fly.

1

To produce a straight shot, your club shaft should parallel the target line at this point in your swing, as in illustration 1.

2

If your club shaft points to the left of target (illustration 2), you will probably swing into the ball from outside the target line and, thus, cut the shot so it slices to the right.

3

If your club shaft points to the right of target (illustration 3), the reverse will normally occur. Your club will move into the ball from the inside and produce a hook spin.

It is possible to hit straight shots from an incorrect position at the top of your swing, but it is impossible to do so with any degree of consistency.

TOP O' THE BACKSWING TO YOU

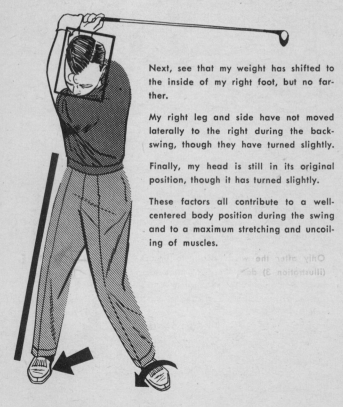

Study the illustration of my top-of-the—swing position and note the four positions that indicate good balance.

Note first that I have rolled to the instep of my forward foot. Yet, I still have this foot fairly well grounded. Many golfers lose balance by going up on this toe.

Next, see that my weight has shifted to the inside of my right foot, but no farther.

My right leg and side have not moved laterally to the right during the backswing, though they have turned slightly.

Finally, my head is still in its original position, though it has turned slightly.

These factors all contribute to a well-centered body position during the swing and to a maximum stretching and uncoiling of muscles.

DON'T LET RIGHT HAND DOMINATE AT TOP OF BACKSWING

At the point shown in illustration 1, a poor-scoring golfer allows his right hand to take over and dominate the downswing. Fight that tendencyl

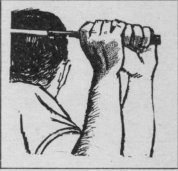

After you reach the top of your backswing, imagine that only your left hand is gripping the club (illustration 2), for this is the hand that guides the club into the downswing.

Only after the wrists begin to uncock (illustration 3) does the right hand take over. This should occur naturally if the left hand has done a good job of guiding.

MAINTAIN A LEFT-SIDE LEAD

1

The phrase "left-side lead" means that, on the downswing, the left side should lead everything else. With a firm left side, you can increase club-head speed and distance.

2

Fortunately, good golfers shift their weight quickly to the left side, thus producing this "left-side lead."

Don't move ahead of the ball on the downswing, as the player in illustration 1 is doing. This weakens the left side and cuts down on consistent accuracy. Instead address the ball on all shots, except with short irons, with your head behind the ball (as in illustration 2) and keep it behind throughout the downswing.

"DELAYED HIT"—A MAJOR SOURCE OF SWING POWER

This illustration of the downswing position shows that my wrists have not uncocked, although my hands have already moved to hip level. I won't unhinge them until my hands have begun to enter the hitting area.

This is known as the "delayed hit," a major source of swing power. A golfer who can reach this "L" position and still square up the club face by impact will certainly hit a long ball.

To reach this position (1) shift your weight to your left at the start of your downswing, (2) lower your right shoulder and return your right elbow to your right side, and (3) avoid forcing the downswing with your hands or swaying your head to your left.

FLYING ELBOW REDUCES POWER AND ACCURACY

It is true that Jack Nicklaus and Gay Brewer have had good success despite a flying right elbow. However, both have outstanding coordination and rhythm. They can return their right elbow to their side early in their downswings without adversely affecting their timing. Most golfers, however, will suffer from an improper swing plane and a premature uncocking of their wrists if they let their elbow fly.

Keep your right elbow in fairly tight as I am doing in illustration 1 and then return it to the right side (illustration 2) at the start of the downswing.

POWERFUL SWING REQUIRES PROPER LEG ACTION

Your legs contain some of the strongest muscles in your body, so let's use this source of power in your swing.

Prober backswing leg action is shown in illustration 1. You will note that, at the top of my backswing, my left knee has moved inward so that it points behind the ball. I have rolled my left foot to its instep. Much of my weight has transferred to the inside of my right foot.

Very early in the downswing (illustration 2), I quickly reverse this leg action. My right knee moves forward toward the ball and my right foot rolls onto the instep. My weight has transferred largely to my left side—but my head remains behind the ball.

The faster your legs can reverse their direction of movement from right to left at the start of your downswing, the more power you will generate for added distance.

RIGHT SHOULDER UNDER

Those who swing their shoulders on a too-level (horizontal) plane usually hit down the left side of the fairway. The principal cause of this is an anxiousness to hit the ball and a resulting too-early use of the right hand on the downswing. As in this illustration, the right shoulder stays much too level on the downswing, moving the club head into the ball in a closed (facing left of the target) position.

As the downswing starts, clamp the right elbow back to the side and move the right shoulder toward a point where it will pass under the chin at impact. The shoulders, in fact, should approximate the intended flight line at this point and even at impact. This helps assure square contact and straight ball flight.

"LEVEL" YOUR RIGHT FOREARM

When I'm hitting the ball, I feel that my right forearm is as level to the ground as possible just before impact. Such action keeps the right elbow in close to the body, thus giving me compact swing and club-head control. A straighter right arm would lead into a loose and ineffective swing.

For power and direction, keep the club head low to the ground for as long as possible after impact.

The "level" right forearm aids in accomplishing this, even though the right arm does naturally straighten at impact. The close-in right elbow will stay just that way, as illustrated, until the ball is well on its way.

AN AID TO GOOD BALANCE

One of the biggest problems golfers face—especially those who take up the game after they have passed their youth—is controlling body weight during the swing. I'd say that more bad swings result from bad balance than from any other single cause.

Balance is often difficult to teach a player, but here is one tip that might help force you to maintain balance during your swing.

The next time you practice, follow my illustrated form and hold your finish position until your shots have landed and stopped bouncing. By doing this you will eventually force yourself to swing in a manner that will allow you to hold your finish. In short, you will force yourself to swing and finish in balance.

The result will be a smoother swing in which you will use your strength to hit the ball, rather than dissipate it in efforts to maintain balance.

TORQUE ACTION INCREASES
CLUB-HEAD SPEED

When your hands move below your belt line on the downswing, you are moving into the all-important hitting area. This is the area in which your club-head speed should be greatest. Your buildup of club-head speed in this area should be gradual; it doesn't help to lunge or jump at the ball.

The increasing club-head speed is derived from what engineers call "torque action," as the body and arms and hands move to the left ahead of the club head. Club-head speed will increase only so long as the hands lead it. Note in the accompanying illustrations how my hands remain ahead of the club head until after impact.

Remember that the hands lead the club head into the ball, but that they must move smoothly without any hint of sudden thrust.

TIP FOR LONGER SHOTS

Look carefully at illustrations 1 and 2. Note that my head and shoulders remain behind the ball throughout the swing, just as they were at address. Note also that this occurs even though much of my weight has moved off my right foot on the downswing.

The ability to "stay behind the ball" in this manner, while still moving weight from right to left on the downswing, can help assure any golfer of increased distance. This action builds up club-head speed and unleashes it into the ball with maximum force.

The golfer who lunges or slides his upper body to the left (illustration 3) sacrifices distance. He weakens his left side and releases his wrists before the club head reaches the ball. Such lateral movement of the head and shoulders also may cause the club head to move outside its proper path. This will result in sliced shots to the right or pulled shots to the left, depending on the direction the club head faces during impact.

HIT STRAIGHTER SHOTS MORE OFTEN

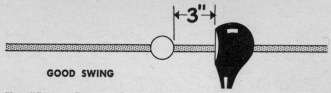

GOOD SWING

The difference between the golfer who hits 50 percent of his shots straight and the golfer who hits only 10 percent straight often boils down to one factor:

Your ability to hit straight shots depends very largely on the distance your club face travels while looking at the target in the hitting area (see illustrations). The longer your club face looks at the target, the better chance you have to hit straight shots. If your club face is turned only one degree off line when it meets the ball, your drives may still finish as much as 25–30 feet to the right or left.

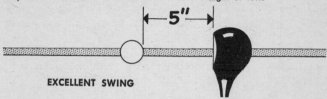

EXCELLENT SWING

Obviously, the object is to keep your club face looking down the target line as long as possible.

The best way to achieve this is to avoid rolling your hands and forearms to the right or left on your backswing.

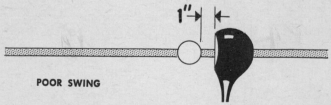

POOR SWING

When you roll them going back, you must perform the exact opposite maneuver on your downswing to return the club face squarely to the ball. This is very difficult to do consistently.

It's much better to take the club back without any independent rolling of your hands.

"HIT DOWN" FOR HEIGHT

It does seem a contradiction in terms to say you must "hit down" when you want the ball to "get up," but that's exactly what must be done.

Notice what happens when you try to lift or scoop the ball up (illustration 1). Such action won't cause the scored club-face markings to rub against the dimpled surface of the ball. Result? Little backspin, a forward movement, but not much rise or height.

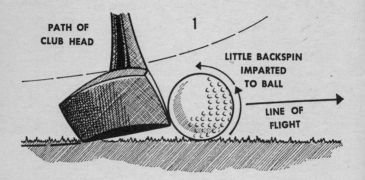

With a down-and-through blow, however (see illustration 2), there's a greater amount of club-ball friction, hence more backspin, height and accuracy.

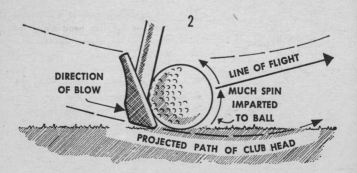

CONTINUE THE CLUB HEAD ALONG TARGET LINE

Shots often stray when you either roll your wrists to the left—closing the clubface—during impact, or move the club face "across the ball" while striking it.

To eliminate these causes of misdirected shots, continue the club head along the target line for an instant longer than normal following impact (see illustration). Don't sway your whole body toward the target; merely throw the club head out along the target line.

Extending the impact zone will automatically give you a full extension of your right arm on the follow-through and a nice, high finish.

PUT YOUR RIGHT HAND TO GOOD USE

Your follow-through and finish are accurate indications of preceding swing actions. Those who don't complete the swing after impact no doubt have slowed down before the ball was struck, robbing themselves of power. Often this takes the form of stopping the swing with the right hand.

Sometimes, we call this the right-hand "clutch." But whatever its name, it's harmful.

Don't allow the right hand to restrict the club head's action through the ball. Feel that its power is being used against a left side firm enough to resist but not stop it. Swing so your hands are well above shoulder level at the finish.

HERE'S TO A HIGH FINISH

A high finish, as shown in illustration 1, is no guarantee of a great shot. But your chances for one improve if you plan from the start to finish in this manner. In order to finish this way, you must move the shoulder down and under—a proper move.

With such a right-shoulder move, the club head will move toward impact from inside to along the target line (see illustration 2). This gives you full shot power and minimizes slicing or pulling, which occurs when the club head moves into the ball from outside the target line.

FLAT FINISHES CAN FINISH YOUR GAME

The flat finish shown in illustration 1 indicates an improper shoulder turn on the downswing that can cause everything from a slice to a pull-hook, depending on the position of the club face at impact. Probably the club head has moved into the ball from outside to inside the target line.

The proper, high finish I demonstrate in illustration 2 indicates a lowering of my right shoulder and a return of my right elbow to my side on the downswing. My club head will have moved into the ball from inside to along the target line. If my club face was facing the target, a straight shot would result.

BUILDING A COMPACT SWING

A swing that is always under control, a swing in which there is no wasted motion—this, to me, is a compact swing, one that gives you the consistent shot control you must have.

For the average golfer, the easiest way to develop this compact swing is to see that the elbows remain consistently close together from address to finish. When the elbows move farther apart than they were at address, the swing becomes loose and sloppy and inconsistent shots result.

In building a compact swing, it also helps to keep your head well-anchored throughout.

BODY TURN AND TILT

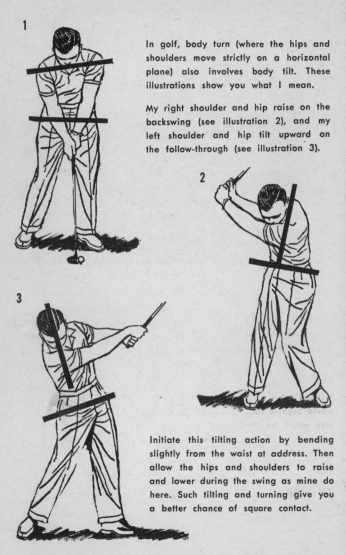

In golf, body turn (where the hips and shoulders move strictly on a horizontal plane) also involves body tilt. These illustrations show you what I mean.

My right shoulder and hip raise on the backswing (see illustration 2), and my left shoulder and hip tilt upward on the follow-through (see illustration 3).

Initiate this tilting action by bending slightly from the waist at address. Then allow the hips and shoulders to raise and lower during the swing as mine do here. Such tilting and turning give you a better chance of square contact.

HEAD TURNS IN BACKSWING
AND DOWNSWING

While it is true that your head should not move laterally or up and down during the swing, the head should rotate, just as the hips and shoulders must, during the swing.

From the illustrations, you can see how and to what extent my head turns or rotates on the backswing and downswing.

Without such head rotation, my swing would become constricted, and the swing arcs would be shortened.

With lateral or up-down head movement, the swing plane and arc would be thrown out of kilter and missed hits would result.

KEEPING THE LEFT ARM STRAIGHT

We've all heard about the importance of a straight left arm in the golf swing. I don't think this aspect of the swing can be overemphasized because the left arm, when properly extended, provides a consistent radius for a consistent swing arc.

I think it might help you keep your left arm straight if you think of it as being a spoke of a wheel.

Think of this spoke as extending from its hub—the left shoulder.

When you make your swing (see illustrations), turn from the "hub" and keep the "spoke" straight.

HOW'S YOUR WEIGHT SHIFT?

At the start of the downswing, the left foot immediately bears most of your weight. If it does not, you're in trouble.

To help this weight shift to the left, get your right knee into the act. Point it toward the ball at address (illustration 1), return it to this position as you go into your downswing (illustration 2), and let it turn with your body on the follow-through.

This action of the right knee, will, with time and practice, force your weight over to the left foot.

LEFT HAND IS KEY TO ACCURACY

The left hand plays a decisive role in determining the direction in which shots will fly.

I suggest that you grip the club so that the back of your left hand points down the target line (illustration 1).

Then during your swing concentrate on returning your left hand to this same position—pointing down the target line—when you strike the ball (illustration 2).

If your club face is properly aligned at address, and if your grip does not loosen during your swing, returning your left hand to its original position should give you proper club-head position during impact. Straighter shots will result.

SWING UNITY PAYS OFF

To bring the big muscles of the back and legs into play, you must swing with the legs, body, shoulders and arms moving together in a unified manner. You will get little help from your back and leg muscles if your hands and arms move the club largely on their own.

To help unify your swing, at address, keep your arms fairly close to your body (see illustration 1). In this way, there is less tendency to start the swing solely with the hands. Instead, the hands will move the club back as your hips and shoulders start turning.

All this unification pays off in the hitting area as your legs and body thrust power through your arms and hands to the club itself (see illustration 2).

HIGH HANDS INDICATE POWERFUL SWING

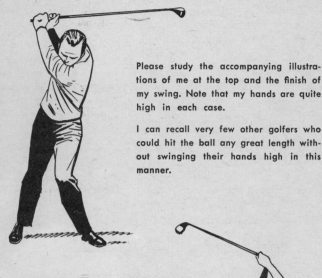

Please study the accompanying illustrations of me at the top and the finish of my swing. Note that my hands are quite high in each case.

I can recall very few other golfers who could hit the ball any great length without swinging their hands high in this manner.

A high hand position on the backswing indicates that the golfer has fully stretched, or coiled, his muscles. It stands to reason that the more fully you stretch your muscles going back, the more power you will generate on your downswing.

A high finish indicates that the golfer has properly lowered his right shoulder on his downswing and thus achieved a "delayed" unhinging of his wrists. It is this delayed hit that produces a full release of maximum club-head speed in the hitting area.

TIMING THE SWING

Very little is written about timing the golf swing. Yet, good timing is a key factor in all successful swings, and the subject certainly merits attention.

Learning to time your golf swing is much like learning to dance. You must swing to a certain rhythm. I happen to have a very fast tempo when swinging. Others, such as Julius Boros, swing to a slower beat. The important thing about timing is not whether you swing slow or fast, but rather that you swing in the same rhythm on all shots with all clubs, from driver to putter.

Naturally, you will swing faster on a drive than you will on a pitch shot, because you take a longer swing with the longer club. The thing to remember is that, though the SPEED of the club head increases with the longer-shafted clubs, the TEMPO or TIMING of the swing remains the same on all normal shots.

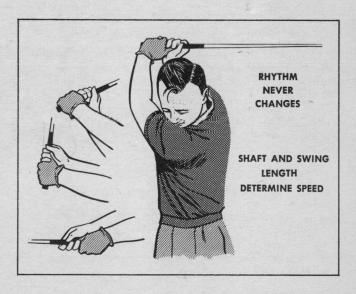

RHYTHM
NEVER
CHANGES

SHAFT AND SWING
LENGTH
DETERMINE SPEED

WEIGHT CENTERED FOR BALANCE

To stay in balance throughout the swing, try to keep your weight centered. Here's what I mean:

At address (see illustration 1), you should feel a downward pressure on the inside of both feet. Also, angle inward with the right knee to keep the weight pressure on the inside of the right foot.

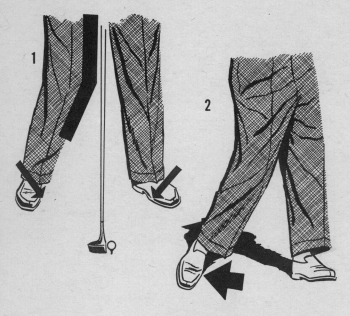

Then, on the downswing (see illustration 2), this inside weight concentration is again pronounced. You push off on the instep and the right knee again angles inward, toward your target.

A TIP TO IMPROVE YOUR SWING BALANCE

I think a big problem that costs shots early in a round of golf is the fact that the player, unaccustomed to swinging a club that day, cannot maintain his best balance on the first few shots.

The obvious way to solve this problem is to hit a bag of balls before each round. But let's be realistic; not all golfers have the time or the inclination to go through a pre-round practice session.

If such is your case, I suggest that before each round you practice-swing a few times with your feet together, as I am doing in the illustrations. This drill forces you to swing slowly and smoothly in order to keep your balance. You can increase the force of your swing as you progress through this drill, but never swing so fast that you lose your balance. After such a drill you can step up to the first tee with muscles loose and your reflexes attuned to a smooth, in-balance swing.

HERE'S CORRECT GOLF-SWING WRIST ACTION

Let there be no independent action of hands and wrists in the golf swing.

Halfway through the backswing (see illustration 1), the palms of both my hands face on a line exactly parallel to the ground. Because they are in this position, I know I haven't twisted my wrists on the backswing.

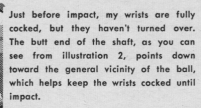

Just before impact, my wrists are fully cocked, but they haven't turned over. The butt end of the shaft, as you can see from illustration 2, points down toward the general vicinity of the ball, which helps keep the wrists cocked until impact.

Halfway through the follow-through, if I were to open my palms, my hands would be perpendicular to the ground—another way of saying that my wrists haven't turned over (see illustration 3).

By aiming for this position, I make sure the club head "follows" the ball after impact for as long as possible, thus giving me accuracy.

EYE FOCUS TIPS

It's all in the mind, of course, but sometimes that golf ball seems to move around at address, doesn't it? This apparent movement is caused by lack of concentration.

At address, pick out an exact spot on the backside of the ball and rivet your eyes to it. Forget the rest of your swing.

Then, as you swing, aim to contact the ball at that point. If you succeed, you'll take a divot in front of the original ball position on all iron shots and many close fairway wood lies.

Imagination plays an important part in golf. Imagine your club head hitting the ball on the backside and chances are you will.

FACTORS DETERMINING YOUR SWING PLANE

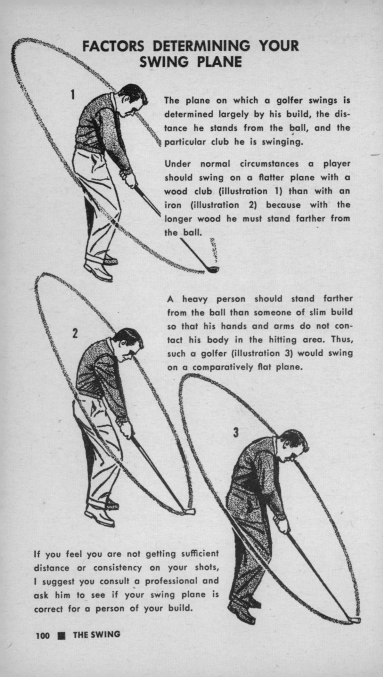

1

The plane on which a golfer swings is determined largely by his build, the distance he stands from the ball, and the particular club he is swinging.

Under normal circumstances a player should swing on a flatter plane with a wood club (illustration 1) than with an iron (illustration 2) because with the longer wood he must stand farther from the ball.

2

A heavy person should stand farther from the ball than someone of slim build so that his hands and arms do not contact his body in the hitting area. Thus, such a golfer (illustration 3) would swing on a comparatively flat plane.

3

If you feel you are not getting sufficient distance or consistency on your shots, I suggest you consult a professional and ask him to see if your swing plane is correct for a person of your build.

"BELT BUCKLE POSITIONS"

Since it is body turn or twist which produces club-head speed—and greater distance—anything to encourage a golfer to pivot well will help. One way to do this is to think of the position of your belt buckle.

At address, it should face just behind the ball for a drive (where the ball is positioned forward). At the top of the backswing it faces the ground behind the ball at a 45-degree angle.

Probably the most important "belt buckle position" is at the finish.

At this point, the buckle should directly face the target. If it heads right of the target, your post-impact turn has been restricted. If it points left, then your swing has probably been too loose for solid contact.

TWO SWING CHECKPOINTS

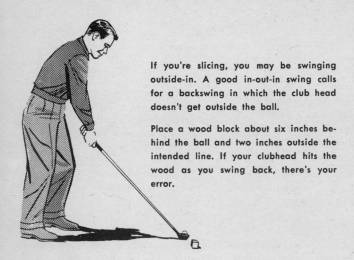

If you're slicing, you may be swinging outside-in. A good in-out-in swing calls for a backswing in which the club head doesn't get outside the ball.

Place a wood block about six inches behind the ball and two inches outside the intended line. If your clubhead hits the wood as you swing back, there's your error.

If you're losing power, you may be swaying as you swing away from the ball. Check this by taking a position with the sun at your back. Then swing at an imaginary ball, but keep your eye on your shadow. It will be easy to see if you're swaying.

Check your putting stroke the same way.

CHAPTER 4

From Driving to Chipping

•

With the fundamentals established, it is now time to turn to the clubs in the golfer's bag—first, to the 13 the player uses to advance the ball from the tee to the green.

Each of these clubs has its own individual characteristics, but, generally speaking, the woods and long irons are designed for distance while the middle and short irons are intended more for short-range accuracy. Of course, the sand wedge has its own specific purpose and doesn't exactly fit into the sequence.

Perhaps the most revealing of the lessons in this chapter is the first one. In it, I show that, even though I have already enjoyed much success on the pro-golf tour, I kept on working hard to improve my game. I discovered that I could drive farther and straighter by teeing the ball up a little higher for my drives and playing the ball a bit more forward in my stance.

Other driving lessons in this chapter stress the need for a sweeping action through the ball, a long, high follow-through, and the need to use common sense when, as is the case most of the time, trouble lies along the path of the drive.

One telling point is made about the fairway woods. While I prefer the long irons to the woods in most situations, I am convinced that the trouble most golfers encounter with fairway woods is mental. I have much the same thing to say about the long irons. In fact, I feel that the golfer should try to think of the woods and long irons as interchangeable clubs, learning to swing them all much the same way.

When the golfer comes to the short irons, he is entering the scoring zone, when a good eight-iron approach, or a lobbed wedge pitch, or a running chip with a five-iron can move the ball close enough to the hole to set up an easy birdie or save a par.

The emphasis in text and illustrations for the short game is on the compactness and restriction of body turn and backswing in these shots. "The Arnold Palmer Method" also encourages the golfer to study the short shots to the greens, as there frequently are several courses of action, and one is usually more effective than the others.

In effect, this chapter tells the golfer how he can save strokes as he approaches the green.

THIS CHANGE RESULTED IN IMPROVED DRIVING

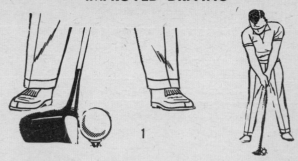

Until about four years ago, I teed my drives only a quarter of an inch above the ground and played the ball well back in my stance (illustration 1). Result? Too much backspin. My drives rose and dropped abruptly. Sometimes my club head dug into the turf. The result was not only a mis-hit shot, but also one that went off-line, for this contact with the ground sometimes opened or closed my club face.

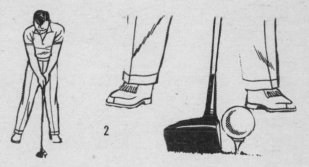

Then I began an experiment that has greatly improved my driving.

I started playing the ball farther forward, opposite my left heel, and teeing it about one inch higher, as shown in illustration 2.

I began hitting the ball either at the bottom of my swing or just after, as the club was starting up. My drives began to shoot out with less backspin. I seldom hit the ground. In effect, I lengthened the interval when my club face was square to the target line. Straighter shots resulted.

PLAY BALL FORWARD AND INCREASE LOFT

You will note in the illustration how the club's loft is reduced when the ball is played back in the stance and struck on the downswing, and how its loft is increased by playing the ball farther forward and hitting it later in the swing.

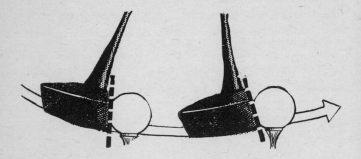

If you have trouble getting your drives off the ground, play the ball farther forward in your stance and tee it higher.

Once this is done, sweep the ball away and up into the air. However, don't try to scoop it up by allowing your weight to remain on your right foot.

FOR BETTER DRIVING

I think most golfers will achieve their best driving accuracy if they address the ball with their feet parallel to the target line (illustration 1). Even if you tend to hook or slice, always maintain a square stance to make sure the club face moves into the ball along the target line. If your normal tendency is to slice, try addressing the ball with your left hip and shoulder turned a bit more to the right. Hookers should turn them to the left. But keep the stance square.

1

2

3

I also advise that you position the ball opposite your left instep (illustration 2) and that you feel the club head sweep the ball off the tee (illustration 3) with the club continuing toward the target well after impact.

GIVE YOURSELF DRIVING ROOM

Sometimes, golfers may become confused about how to position the club at address for a full drive.

One checkpoint is this: Most players will be in good position if the butt end of the shaft is about 4 inches from the body at address. The golfer is thus neither cramped nor extended.

With the ball played too close to the feet, the distance between the end of the grip and the body is drastically reduced. It's easy to see how this could cramp the swing.

But there is danger the other way, too. With the hands too far out, the golfer will swing much too flat and probably come up on his toes at impact.

ADDRESS YOUR DRIVES CORRECTLY

The player in illustration 1 has positioned his ball too far back for a drive.

Because of this bad positioning, the club face will contact the ball, as in illustration 2, before it can return to its square-

to target position. The face is pointed to the right of the target—and that's the direction the ball will take.

Avoid this risk of slicing by playing the ball farther forward in the stance (see illustration 3). At contact, the club face will have a better chance to reach the ball squarely.

DRIVE AWAY FROM TROUBLE

Most golfers cannot count on a straight tee shot most of the time. Yet, these same players fail to take heed to an important golf maxim when they drive on holes guarded by trouble. This maxim is: "Always drive away from trouble."

In other words, tee up on the side of the tee that is closest to the trouble. If you see rough or out-of-bounds on the right, drive from the right side of the tee. However, aim for the center of the fairway, rather than down the right side. Thus, a sliced shot will have to bend at a much sharper angle to reach the trouble than it would have to if you had hit straight down the fairway from the middle of the tee.

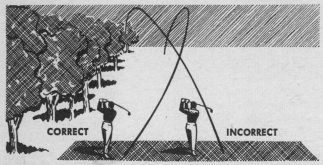

The opposite holds true when there is trouble on the left. Drive from the left side of the tee and aim for the middle, rather than down the left side.

Remember: Always shoot away from trouble.

WHEN THE WIND BLOWS

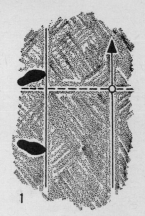

Here are a few tips that will help you counteract the effect of the wind on your tee shots. Let's assume that you normally play the ball opposite your left heel when driving (illustration 1).

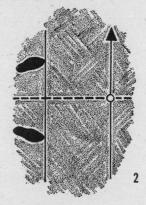

When hitting into the wind, play the ball farther back in your stance (illustration 2). This will cut down the loft on your driver at impact and produce a low, "wind-cheating" shot.

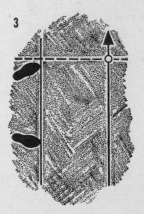

If the wind is with you, play the ball farther forward than normally (illustration 3). This will give you a high shot and maximum distance.

For best distance in a crosswind, merely aim to the side of the fairway from which the wind is blowing. Let the wind work for you by carrying the ball to the middle. Don't attempt intentionally to slice or hook into the wind. This will only minimize your distance.

FINESSING WITH THE 4-WOOD

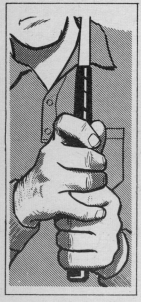

In recent years we have seen a minor development in golf: the tendency for average- and high-handicap golfers to substitute 5-, 6- and even 7-wood clubs where normally they would use a 2-, 3-, or 4-iron. Personally, I can better control a long iron than a lofted wood club, but I see nothing wrong with golfers hitting these woods if they have trouble with their long irons.

However, you are allowed only 14 clubs —and no substitutes during a round.

Actually, the 4-wood can be made to function like a 4-iron. It's very simple. All you must do is choke up on the grip three or four inches (see illustration). Then swing just as you would on a normal 4-wood shot. By "shortening" the club shaft in this manner, you will automatically shorten the length of your swing and the distance of the shot.

CONTROLLING THE FAIRWAY WOODS

I have felt for a long time that too many club golfers waste too many strokes on their fairway-wood shots.

I think part of the problem is mental. Often, on a fairway-wood shot, the golfer is striving to do something that extends beyond his normal limits. He might be trying to reach a par-5 hole in two, or he might be trying to gain a few more yards by swinging a 2-wood, when a 4-wood would be a much safer club for the close lie at hand.

The result of all this is that some golfers

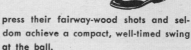
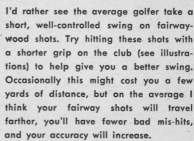

press their fairway-wood shots and seldom achieve a compact, well-timed swing at the ball.

I'd rather see the average golfer take a short, well-controlled swing on fairway-wood shots. Try hitting these shots with a shorter grip on the club (see illustrations) to help give you a better swing. Occasionally this might cost you a few yards of distance, but on the average I think your fairway shots will travel farther, you'll have fewer bad mis-hits, and your accuracy will increase.

SWEEP THE LONG IRONS

Long-iron (Nos. 1, 2 & 3) technique is decidedly specialized. The long-iron swing is a sweeping motion, rather than the downward action used for shorter clubs.

First, play the ball forward, off your left instep. Then take a full pivot, or body turn, as you swing back.

The ball is contacted slightly on the upswing in a long-iron shot. As in every other golf shot except the sand explosion, it must be contacted first. But the swing path isn't down and through, but "up" and through.

The best long-iron golfers take only a small divot after impact.

HELP FOR THE LONG IRONS

Most golfers have trouble with long-iron shots. Even many good players will "choke up" on a 4-wood rather than chance swinging a 2-iron.

I think that much of the problem with long irons is mental. Golfers fear the 2- and 3-irons so they naturally have trouble. Assuming the problem is largely mental, let's try using the mind—specifically your imagination—to eliminate the phobia.

I suggest you think of your long irons as being no different than the wood club —say the 4-wood—that you hit best. Then, whenever you swing a 2- or 3-iron, imagine that you are swinging a 4-wood. Consciously try to imitate the stance, ball positioning and actual swing of the 4-wood. Sweep the ball off the grass just as you would with the wood. Actually there is so little difference between the fairway-wood and long-iron swings that you will be giving your shots a proper stroke— and you will be doing it in a positive frame of mind.

LONG-IRON GUIDE

Long irons (the 2 and 3) may be more difficult to use with success for the average golfer, but they're great for checking your swing. If you've developed incorrect habits, take your long irons to the practice tee. Once you get them going well, then swings with your other clubs will fall into place.

For one thing, check your left-hand grip at the top of the swing—it should be snug, as illustrated.

If your right elbow tends to "fly" on the downswing, blame the overpowering right hand.

At any rate, clamping the right elbow back down to the side at backswing start will keep the club head on a good swing arc. Moving the hands towards the ground will keep them ahead of the club head, and will eventually help square the club face at impact.

ON ALL IRON SHOTS, THE WORD IS "TEMPO"

Too many golfers swing harder and faster on long-iron shots than on short shots.

When you try to swing fast, you're putting too much emphasis on your arm muscles. Let your hips, legs and feet get into the act and do the job of generating long-iron power.

5-IRON

2-IRON

In short, swing your long irons in the same tempo you use on short-iron shots. Bring the lower half of your body into more play as you progress to the longer clubs. Remember, your clubs have built-in characteristics that will make them perform properly. Just let them do their job; swing them all in the same tempo.

KEEP THOSE IRON SHOTS UNDER CONTROL

An iron shot's sole function is accuracy, yet many golfers insist on going for distance as well. They overswing and sacrifice accuracy.

In the illustration, we see two lengths of backswing with a 5-iron. The proper length of backswing varies with the individual. I will suggest, however, that most golfers in the middle- and high-handicap range would score lower if they shortened their backswing on iron shots.

A shorter backswing with the irons need not cut your distance. Most golfers can generate just as much distance-producing club-head speed—and much better accuracy—with a shorter, well-controlled swing.

ACCURACY WITH THE IRONS

Even low-handicap players occasionally run into periods when they lose the ability to hit consistently iron shots on target. When this happens to me, the first thing I do is to check my follow-through. It may sound as if I'm putting the cart before the horse to do this, but often, if I can correct my follow-through position, the original cause of the inaccurate shots will automatically disappear.

On the follow-through, your hands should move out toward the target, then up and around, pulling your body up (illustration 1).

If I have been pushing my iron shots to the right of target, it may be that I'm quitting on my follow-through, as in illustration 2. If my irons shots are pulling

to the left, it may be because I have insufficient weight on my left leg at the finish of the swing (illustration 3).

Altering your follow-through will not, in itself, improve your shot results. However, it may force you to correct earlier errors that have caused the trouble.

KEEP MIDDLE IRONS UNDER CONTROL

The good middle-iron (5, 6, 7) player can make well-positioned drives pay off.

I like to open my stance a bit on these shots, to get a freer, easier backswing movement. Aim for the big part of the green under normal circumstances and start back slowly, deliberately.

The hands should get only a bit above shoulder height on a mid-iron shot. Power isn't the No. 1 aim in this shot; direction is. And the shorter and more controlled the backswing, the straighter your shot.

Experts keep the left heel on the ground in the backswing, although they do roll the foot over. Most weight should be felt on the inside of the right foot at this point.

SHORT BACKSWING FOR SHORT SHOTS

A common fault among novice golfers is taking much too long a backswing on shots from within, say, 40 yards of the green. After taking a long backswing, they let the club head "coast" into the ball. In short, such golfers are regulating the length of the shot by the force of the swing, rather than its length.

Failure to accelerate the club head into the ball produces sloppiness and loss of club control. Scuffed or topped shots result.

In the illustrations I am hitting a wedge shot of about 30 yards. Note that my backswing is short—the hands barely reach hip height—and then I gradually accelerate the speed of the club head as it moves into and through the ball.

Learn to regulate the distance you hit these shots by the length of your backswing. Thus, you will be able to strike at the ball with about the same force on all shots, regardless of their length. Not only will you hit these shots more squarely, but you will also develop a more sensitive touch.

CHIPPING AND PUTTING ARE SIMILAR

Because the two strokes have much in common, a good chipper should not be a poor putter, and vice versa.

The illustrations show me at the finish of a long putt (25 feet or more) and a chip from just off the green. Note the similarity of positions.

In both shots, the eyes should be over the ball, weight shaded to the left, feet square to the line. Only the arms and shoulders should be used in the stroke. Restrict body motion.

If you finish both shots as illustrated—with the club face square to the target—you'll improve in each department.

INCREASING PRECISION ON SHORT SHOTS

Accuracy is the prime goal on short shots to the green. The good golfer does everything he can to keep his swing simple on such shots so that he can expect straight shots.

In the illustrations I am demonstrating how to execute a full shot with the pitching wedge. I would like you to pay special attention to my left heel.

You will note that this heel remains firmly planted throughout the swing, though my

legs move and my hips and shoulders tilt and turn.

I feel that, by keeping this heel on the ground, I eliminate one more moving part from my overall swing machinery. This decreases the chance for error and increases chances that my club head will

return to the ball squarely, facing in the same direction it was in at address.

It may be necessary for some golfers to raise their left heel on longer shots in order to make a full backswing, but as a long backswing is not necessary—or even desirable—on short shots, I think everyone will get better accuracy by keeping the left heel firmly planted throughout.

ON SHORT SHOTS, WRISTS COCK EARLIER

On the backswing, the wrists should cock automatically when the hands reach about hip height.

However, the wrists do cock earlier on short shots than on shots with the woods and long irons. You will note in the illustrations that, though my hands are about at a similar height, the wrist cock is much more noticeable on the short-iron shot.

On long shots there is more emphasis on distance. Therefore you need a wider swing arc. The hands and arms should push the club away from the body on the backswing, even if the right elbow must move away from the right side. All this results in a later cocking of the wrists.

On short shots, you want accuracy and a more compact swing. The right elbow should remain close to your side for a more upright backswing and earlier wrist-cocking.

FOR BETTER CHIP SHOTS

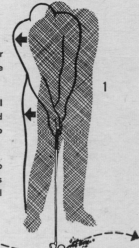

There is really no reason to move your body on short chip shots from around the edge of a green.

For accuracy, follow the same advice I give in putting: keep your head and body still. Let your arms and hands do the work.

The golfer who shifts his body laterally to the rear on short shots (illustration 1) is liable to strike the turf behind the ball and "poop" the shot.

If a player moves his body forward with the club on such shots (illustration 2), he may strike too high on the ball. This is called "blading the shot."

If you keep your body steady, your chances of returning the iron to its original position, under the ball, will be improved. Just brush the turf with your iron and sweep the ball away.

ON SHORT SHOTS, WEIGHT STAYS TO LEFT

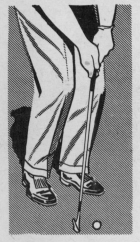

On chip shots from around the edge of a green, we must make certain that the club does not strike the ground before it meets the ball.

The best way to avoid such scuffed shots is to address the ball with your hands slightly ahead of the ball and with most of your weight on your left foot (illustration 1).

Then keep your weight on your left foot throughout your chipping stroke (illustrations 2 and 3).

Keeping your weight to the left will cause your club to brush the grass and sweep the ball into the air. Only when your hands move behind the ball or your weight shifts to the right will you be in danger of scuffing the shot.

CHIP WITH FIRM LEFT WRIST

1

Say the word "chip" to yourself. It sounds quick and sharp; there is, nothing soft about it. The chip shot in golf should be played just as the word sounds. There should be nothing soft or lazy about your chip shot stroke.

The best way to make your chip shots crisp is to keep the left wrist firm throughout the shot. Never let it get flabby so that it bends or buckles as in illustration 1.

Address the ball with your left wrist firm and slightly ahead of the ball as in illustration 2. Maintain this firmness on the backstroke (illustration 3). Then strike the ball with your hands and wrists in approximately the same position as they were at address in illustration 2.

2

3

The firm left wrist will give you the solid contact with a square club face that is so necessary, especially on short shots where accuracy is of utmost importance.

THINK "WHISK" ON CHIP SHOTS

Sometimes words sound like what they describe. A case in point is the broom. Anyone who's used one knows that it says "whisk" when you sweep with it.

I think "whisk" is a good sound to think about when you make a chip shot from the edge of a green. The club head should brush the grass and "whisk" the shot away. There is nothing lazy or sloppy about a good chip shot. It's quick and firm. It "whisks."

So make your chip shots "whisk." In fact, you might even imagine that you are swinging a broom (see illustration).

HOW TO HIT A "SOFT" WEDGE SHOT

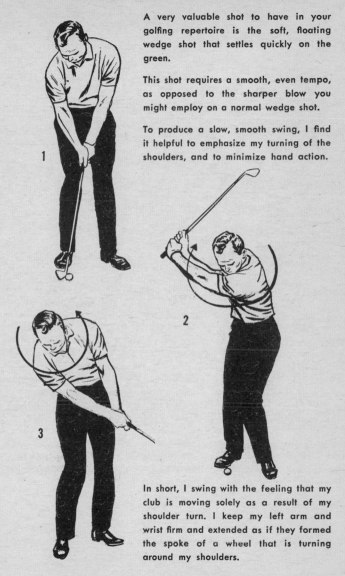

A very valuable shot to have in your golfing repertoire is the soft, floating wedge shot that settles quickly on the green.

This shot requires a smooth, even tempo, as opposed to the sharper blow you might employ on a normal wedge shot.

To produce a slow, smooth swing, I find it helpful to emphasize my turning of the shoulders, and to minimize hand action.

In short, I swing with the feeling that my club is moving solely as a result of my shoulder turn. I keep my left arm and wrist firm and extended as if they formed the spoke of a wheel that is turning around my shoulders.

PITCHING WEDGE—A STROKE SAVER

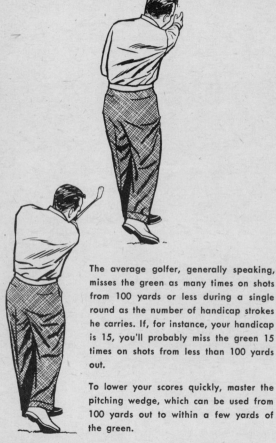

The average golfer, generally speaking, misses the green as many times on shots from 100 yards or less during a single round as the number of handicap strokes he carries. If, for instance, your handicap is 15, you'll probably miss the green 15 times on shots from less than 100 yards out.

To lower your scores quickly, master the pitching wedge, which can be used from 100 yards out to within a few yards of the green.

With this club, use a "swinging" stroke instead of a "slopping" one. Execute it the way you would toss a ball underhand.

Minimize body and leg movement and be sure the club head contacts the ball before the turf.

"LOB PITCH" A HANDY SHOT

Scarcely a round of golf goes by in which the player doesn't have at least one occasion to use the "lob pitch."

This short shot is used when the player has very little green between his ball and the hole—or if the green is very fast or runs downhill away from him.

The lob shot is handy at such times because this shot floats high through the air, drops almost vertically and settles quickly on the green.

You should use either a 9-iron or a pitching wedge for this shot. Play the ball well forward in your stance (illustration 1). The object is to have the club head slide under the ball. This differs from the normal pitch shot, which requires a down-

ward blow on the ball, which flies lower than the lob and which carries more backspin.

On the lob shot, your backswing should be longer than for a normal pitch of the same length (illustration 2). Keep your swing smooth and easy throughout and be sure you finish the shot as I have (illustration 3).

HOW TO CHIP YOUR WAY OUT
OF TROUBLE

The chip is a handy, low, rolling shot.

A straight-faced club controls it, such as a 2- or 3-iron when you're within 6 feet of the green's edge. Move to more lofted clubs for farther distances.

1

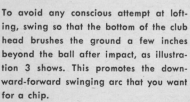

Ilustration 2 points up the fact that there's no wrist-twisting on the chip's backswing. For maximum control, choke down on the grip a couple of inches and let the club loft the ball.

2

To avoid any conscious attempt at lofting, swing so that the bottom of the club head brushes the ground a few inches beyond the ball after impact, as illustration 3 shows. This promotes the downward-forward swinging arc that you want for a chip.

3

HIGH-LOFTED PITCH TO GREEN HAS UNDESIRABLE EFFECT

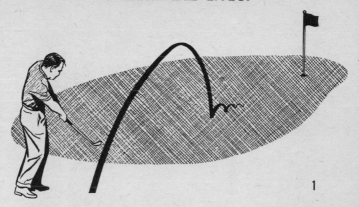

1

Whenever you're a few yards from the edge of a green and the terrain between your ball and the hole is fairly normal, don't take a chance on trying to pitch with a highly lofted club.

On such a short shot, a wedge or 9-iron will cause the ball to fly high with a lot of backspin. When it hits the green, it "grabs" far short of the hole (see illustration 1).

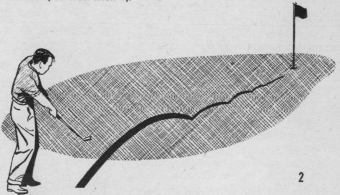

2

Far better to chip with a middle iron, such as a 5 or 6. Such a chip will bounce and roll to the hole, even if it isn't struck perfectly square. Pick the spot on the green from which your ball will bounce and roll to the hole; then try to land your chip near that spot.

PLANNING A SHORT SHOT FROM THE EDGE OF A GREEN

If your ball has settled low in the grass, but still rests on grass (see illustration 1), expect a low-flying shot. Chip with a more lofted club to get height and to dig the ball out easily.

Conversely, a ball that sits high in the grass (see illustration 2) will be a "high flyer," so it's wiser to chip with a less lofted club to cut down the height.

Now, note illustration 3. Here the ball rests between grass, but still on bare ground. From this lie, stick with a straighter-faced club, such as a 5- or 6-iron. Pop the ball out, by using a firm, sharply descending swing.

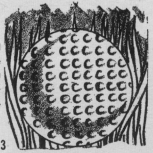

BACK-UP TO LOWER SCORES

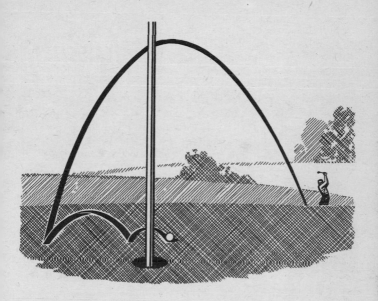

The handy back-up shot, illustrated, must be of about 90 or 100 yards in length, so that it enables you to take a full swing with a highly lofted club, such as a fairway wedge.

Also, the ball should be lying on firm ground in order to make the back-up a successful shot.

Position the ball well back in your stance and keep as much of your body weight on your left foot as possible throughout the swing. Lift the club abruptly on the backswing and return it to the ball with a sharp downward movement. The club will lend backspin to the ball as it slides up the face of the club.

Since the club must cut down and through the turf, keep a firm left-hand grip.

SOME WEDGE SHOT POINTERS

Let's say you're positioned just off the edge of a green and you can't chip with a 6- or 7-iron because the pin is too close. Your best bet in this case is a short and soft wedge chip. The ball must land on the green and stop quickly before it goes way past the hole.

Use the wedge but swing as though you were chipping. And, to increase the club's loft for a high shot that settles quickly, lay back the blade at address.

Here are some other pointers: Strike the ball with a slightly downward blow, keep your hands ahead of the ball, and be sure you keep a firm left wrist.

WHICH CLUB TO USE ON SHORT SHOTS

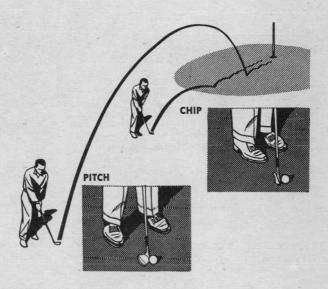

PITCH

CHIP

Whenever you are close enough to the green so that you can chip the ball low with a 5-, 6-, 7-, or 8-iron so that it lands on the green and doesn't roll past the hole, go ahead and do so.

On longer shots, where these clubs would not stop a ball that landed on the green before it went way past the hole, you must use a more lofted club—a wedge or 9-iron—and pitch the ball high to land close to the hole.

Normally, the chip shot is easier to make safely than is the pitch. So use this shot unless it is absolutely necessary to pitch the ball high. However, always try to land the ball on the smooth putting surface no matter which shot you are playing.

TREAT THIS SHORT APPROACH AS A CHIP

Suppose you're facing a short approach shot and your ball is resting on bare ground. The thing to do is to play the shot as a normal chip.

Use a less-lofted iron (illustration 1) and play the shot to run onto the green. Keep your hands ahead of the club head, contact the ball before the ground, and keep a steady head.

1

2

Too many golfers try to pitch such shots with a highly lofted club (illustration 2) and wind up with a "skulled" or "bladed" shot.

Further, if there's no hazard or deep grass between you and the green (and if you practice plenty), you might find that the putter is a handy club for such shots.

SHORT CUT TO SHORT-IRON ACCURACY

Take your wedge or 9-iron and line up three balls in a row (see illustration). Practice trying to make all three balls fly on the same shot.

To make this trick shot work, you must strike the first ball while your club head is descending—just before it reaches the bottom of its arc.

This is the same technique all good golfers employ on short-iron shots. They always "hit down" on the ball, contacting the ball first and then the turf.

If you practice this trick shot until you have it mastered, I'm sure your short-iron game will improve immensely.

WET-WEATHER CHIP

Here are some wet-weather chipping pointers:

As the greens will be damp, expect less roll than usual. Thus, you'll want to land the ball closer to the hole than normal. For a 40-foot chip, I'd say use a 7-iron and try to drop the ball 10 feet in front of the cup.

Normally, you'd use a 5-iron for this shot and try to land the ball about 20 feet from the cup and depend on roll for the remaining distance. This won't work in wet weather.

Because you want a lot of roll and control, play the ball farther forward than usual and swing the club head low to the ground after impact.

PRACTICE YOUR SHORT GAME

As any golfer can cut his scores quickly with an improvement in his short game, it's wise to get those short sticks to the practice range often. Here's a plan: Hit 50-yard wedge shots until you can put 10 straight on the green, then 5 or 10 within 10 feet of the cup.

Then move up to the green and chip from 20 feet away. Practice landing the ball on the green until you can put eight of 10 shots within 3 feet of the cup.

Then try 30-foot putts until you can get 8 of 10 within a foot of the cup.

CHAPTER 5

Putting

•

Many pro golfers wince when described as good putters. They seem to think that, because they are called good putters, it automatically follows that they are branded as bad players. Yet all knowledgeable golfers will agree that, if you are not putting well, you are not scoring. Putting is far too important a part of the game to suffer neglect.

As the putting stroke is relatively simple, many players spend most, if not all, of their practice time hitting balls with the other clubs. They fail to remember that half of the strokes allotted for a round of golf are expected to occur on the greens. Realizing this fact, the smart golfer concentrates on developing a personalized putting touch that will truly cut down his score.

Nothing in golf is more individualistic than putting.

Certain rules apply to all—the firmness of the head, the low, straight takeaway, the square contact with the ball. On the other hand, there is no universally accepted grip (although, as I point out in one lesson of this chapter, most pros employ similar grips or one prescribed stance, or any hard and fast principles governing the position of the head or hands in relation to the ball. In fact, a cross-section study of the present pro tour will reveal styles that veer far, far from the conventional. Some pros swing the putter like a pendulum, either between the legs with the golfer facing the hole, or in the usual sidesaddle fashion. Others have enjoyed considerable success using a cross-handed grip.

But the factor that makes putting so completely individualistic is precision. In no other phase of the game is the golfer required to be so precise with the direction and distance of his shot. No player can teach another person how hard to hit a putt in an exact direction. This is something each golfer must learn for himself from constant trial and error on and off the course.

Certain of the lessons in this chapter contain tips that should make the development of this touch easier. Others should help the inexperienced golfer understand why certain things happen to a ball as it rolls across the putting surface, why one putt will curve more than another on a similar slope, why a putt from one direction on a green will roll farther and faster than one from the opposite direction.

The next time you attend a pro golf tournament, notice how crowded the putting green is practically all day every day. The pros know what a good, confident putting stroke can do for their scores.

A PUTTING GRIP THAT WORKS

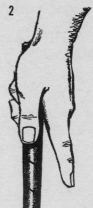

The favorite putting grip of the touring pros is called the "reverse overlap" grip. Here is how it works.

Illustrations 1 and 2 show the left hand from a side and a front view respectively. Note that the club is held largely in the fingers to promote a maximum sense of "feel."

The thumb extends down the top of the shaft and the forefinger extends down the side. Thus the back of this hand faces the target line.

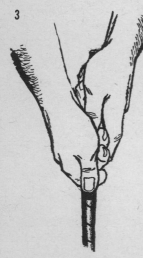

When the right hand is added (illustration 3), we see that this thumb also extends down the top of the shaft. The hands are combined snugly together so that the forefinger of the left laps over the fingers of the right.

When the hands are combined in this manner, they will work together as a unit. The palms face each other and most of the gripping is done in the fingers. I feel this is the putting grip that best provides proper direction and sensitivity in the hands.

PUTTING STYLES VARY

Of all phases of golf none has more leeway for individualism than does putting.

You will note my putting position in illustration 1 finds my knees and elbows in tight. This "locked" position helps me keep from moving my body or head during the stroke.

Whereas I keep my head over the ball, Jack Nicklaus, who is an excellent putter (illustration 2), positions his head well behind the ball.

Doug Sanders (illustration 3) uses a much narrower stance than does Nicklaus and employs a longer stroke than I do.

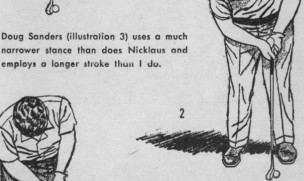

Regardless of your style, however, I do think it is important that you be as still as possible during your stroke and that you accelerate your putter into the ball so that you strike it soundly and squarely.

Once you find a putting style that produces a consistent and sure stroke, I think you should stick with it, even if you occasionally have a bad day on the greens.

THE PUTTING PICTURE

1

In my style of putting, I never allow my left wrist to hinge or break after impact. I see to it that the left hand leads the stroke, so that my right hand never gets a chance to take over and, thus, to close the blade of the putter on the through stroke.

2

In this way, also, I keep the blade accelerating way past the point of impact for a firm, decisive stroke.

3

Look at the illustrations; my right hand, you'll see, never passes my left.

BE A "SQUARE"

To become a consistently good putter, you must stroke your putts so that the club face is moving along the target line as you strike the ball.

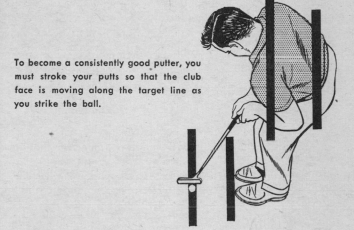

The surest way to achieve such a putting stroke is to make certain that your feet, knees, hips and shoulders are all positioned to parallel the target line (see illustration). If you are fully positioned square to the target in this manner, it will be difficult for you to err in your putting stroke. More solidly stroked putts will result from this proper address position.

A PROPER PATH
FOR YOUR PUTTER

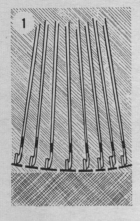

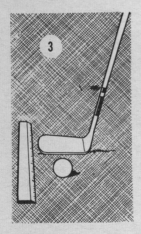

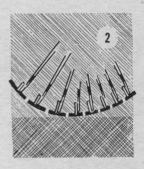

On all golf shots it is important that your club head move along a proper path. This is especially true when putting.

Your putter should go back and through the ball low to the ground (illustration 1) to strike the ball squarely. Abruptly lifting the blade on the back or through stroke (illustration 2) may cause you to stub or top the putt. It may also cause the ball to skid, rather than to roll, off the putter face. This makes it difficult to get a true roll on the putt.

Also, you should try to move the putter head straight back and through the ball. Never slice the putt by letting the blade move to the outside on the backstroke. Taking the blade back and forth along a ruler (illustration 3) will help promote the straight-back, straight-through idea in your mind.

PUTTING STROKE ACCELERATES

Tempo is just as important in the putting stroke as it is in the full swing with a driver. In putting, the tempo should be smooth and it should accelerate.

Your putter should start back slowly and then gradually move faster through a stroke so that it is moving fastest as it meets the ball.

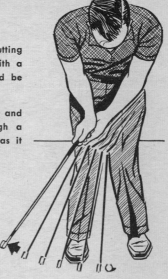

You cannot expect to putt well unless your putter is accelerating at point of contact. Only with this acceleration will the blade remain square to the target line throughout the time that it is moving the ball.

If your putts are erratic in their line, especially if you have a tendency to "pull" your putts to the left, I suggest you make sure that your putter is accelerating through the ball and that you are following through on the stroke toward the target with your putter head.

WATCH PUTTER
STRIKE THE BALL

I think that more putts are missed (especially the short ones) because the player moves his head during the stroke than for any other single reason. I have fallen into this habit myself. In fact, I won the 1962 British Open only after my wife, Winnie, pointed out this failing to me during a practice round prior to the tournament.

When you move your head during your putting stroke, not only is the rhythm of your stroke destroyed, but also the putter's alignment to the target line is adversely affected.

The best advice I can give to preserve a steady head is actually to watch the putter strike the ball. This, in itself, requires a certain amount of concentration, and this forced attention helps eliminate any anxiety that might cause you to lift your head prematurely.

USE LONG STROKES ON LONG PUTTS

Many golfers use approximately the same length of putting stroke on all putts, regardless of their distance. I think this is a mistake.

If you use a short stroke on long putts, you will have to increase the force of your stroke to get the ball to the hole. When you increase the force or speed of your stroke, it often becomes rushed or jerky. Good timing is just as vital on putts as it is on tee shots.

Try to stroke all of your putts with the same rhythm. When you have a long putt, merely make a longer stroke, as I am doing in the illustration. If the rhythm of your putting stroke remains consistent on all putts, your pattern of putting results also should become more consistent.

PUTTING SIMPLIFIED

There are many things that a golfer can think about during his putting stroke—"Keep the head still," "Take the club straight back," "Accelerate the stroke." These are all good reminders, but to think about so many points during such a short time is apt to hinder the rhythm of your stroke.

After the player has set himself up in a comfortable address position (illustration 1), I think he would be wise to concentrate on no more than one stroke fundamental.

The fundamental you choose will probably vary from time to time. However, during the stroke (illustrations 2 and 3), I suggest you try thinking only about contacting the ball as squarely as possible. When your thinking is directed to this single goal, you will find that other stroke fundamentals, such as keeping the head still, will occur automatically.

A QUICK WAY TO GUIDE PUTTING STROKE

If you have ever wondered why professional golfers seem so meticulous about how they replace a ball on the putting green, this may answer your question.

Naturally, we always try to replace the ball in exactly the same spot it occupied before we marked it. However, some players go a step further. They not only place the ball on exactly the same spot, but they also place it in a manner so that the name on the ball points directly along the desired line to the hole (illustration 1).

1

2

The reason for positioning the ball in this manner should be obvious. If the lettering on the ball points the way to the target, then all the player must do is to make his back and through stroke follow an imaginary extension of this lettering (illustration 2).

If the stroke is so executed, the ball will roll along the desired line and will have an excellent chance of dropping.

A CURE FOR PUSHED PUTTS

1

One of the prime requirements for consistently successful putting is that the golfer's body remain still during the stroke. Once his body moves, he loses control of the club-face position.

A common body movement in putting is the sliding of the hips toward the hole as the putter moves into the ball (illustration 1). Such movement usually opens the club face so that the putt is pushed out to the right of the intended line.

2

To eliminate any such movement during my putting stroke, I stand over the ball with my knees firmly locked together (illustration 2). By prelocking myself in this position before I putt, I find it easier to stroke the ball solely through hand and arm movement.

Again, the fewer moving parts you must control, the better your chances for consistent accuracy—and on no shot is accuracy more important than on the putt.

A CURE FOR OFF-LINE PUTTING

Obviously, your putter face must be looking down your intended line when it meets the ball. Otherwise, your putts are not going to have much chance of dropping.

Yet, many golfers fail to stroke their putts on line because they allow their left wrist to start collapsing before the ball is on its way (see illustration). Unless your left wrist remains firm, the club face will be turned to your left when it meets the ball. This will cause you to pull your putts. It may, over a period of time, cause you to start compensating by pushing them to the right.

CORRECT

INCORRECT

Simply grip your putter so that the back of your left hand faces down the target line. Keep it facing down this line both on your back and on your through stroke. If the back of this hand moves through the ball along the line, your putter will face down the same line (see illustration).

PROPERLY POSITIONING THE BALL ON PUTTS

Most golfers have mastered the technique of "playing the ball off the high foot" on uphill and downhill lies in the fairway. Because of the upward or downward slope, they play the ball more forward or farther back, always toward the higher foot. This change in ball position automatically adjusts a golfer's swing to compensate for the irregular terrain.

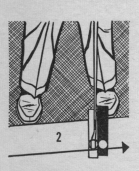

NORMAL POSITION

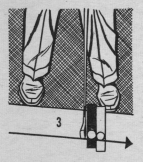

NORMAL POSITION

If a golfer makes this change in ball positioning on fairway shots, it stands to reason that he should also make some compensation, though not to such a degree, on uphill and downhill putts.

If you position the ball for level putts off your left instep as I do (illustration 1), I suggest you play putts from uphill lies off your left toe (illustration 2). Play downhill putts about an inch farther back than normal (illustration 3).

You will find that this alteration in the ball's position will help give you more solid contact on the putt.

STRIKE THE BALL ON SWEET SPOT
OF PUTTER FACE

The spot on the putter face where it strikes the ball makes a great deal of difference in the success of your putting. All clubs, including putters, have a "sweet spot." This is the spot at which a ball, meeting the face, will not open or close it.

Hold your putter at its grip end lightly between the thumb and forefinger of one hand. Then, tap the putter face with a finger of your other hand. When you tap and the putter face doesn't open or close but jumps straight back, you have found its sweet spot.

Then when you putt, play the ball just opposite this sweet spot and strike it there. This will give you solid putts that won't pull to the left or push to the right because of a turning putter head.

PUTTING FROM THE FRINGE

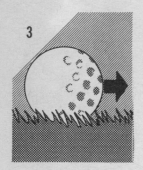

Many average golfers are better with a putter than they are with a chipping club. Yet, these same players will often refuse to putt from just off the green because they feel the "correct" shot from such position is the chip.

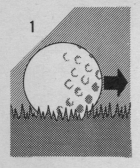

Let me say right here and now that the so-called correct shot in any situation is the one that will give you the best results. Never feel guilty about putting from off the green, if you feel the putter will give you the best chance for a successful shot.

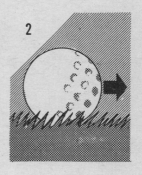

Bear in mind, however, that putts from the fringe will be most successful if the ball is resting on short grass (illustration 1) or if the grass lays toward the hole (illustration 2). If the grass lays away

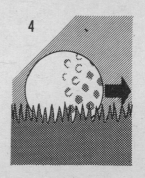

from the green (illustration 3) or if your ball is nestled into the grass (illustration 4), you will probably be better off if you chip it out and onto the green with a 5-iron or 6-iron.

PUTTING UNDER PRESSURE

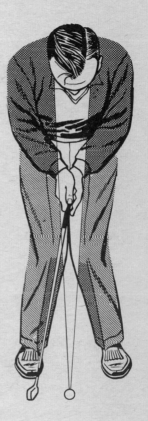

When the chips are down and you must sink a putt, it is helpful to have one positive key thought that will close your mind to any fear of missing.

One good key thought for any golfer is merely to strike the ball squarely. Focus your attention on the back of the ball and think only of giving it a firm rap (see illustration). This will not only take your mind off the possibility of missing, but it will also cause your head to remain motionless throughout the stroke.

Some golfers become so tense under pressure that they cannot take the putter back smoothly. If this happens to you, merely loosen your grip on the club slightly and, again, concentrate on striking the putt squarely.

HOW I LINE UP PUTTS

There really is no "right" way to plan putts. It all depends on the individual. Personally, I prefer to first look at the putt from each side, then from behind the ball.

Looking at it from the sides gives me an idea of the general direction the putt will break. I make sure that I look at the line from BOTH sides. If I look at it from only the low side of the line (figure at right in illustration), I tend to overestimate the amount of slope.

Sizing up the putt from behind the ball gives me my specific line. Of course, I'm considering whatever I might have noticed from the sides.

In selecting the line for a putt, you must also imagine how fast you will be expecting the ball to travel. Obviously you can expect less break when you "charge" the hole than when you plan to have the ball "die" at the cup.

Whenever possible, line up your putt while your fellow players are putting. If all golfers would do this one simple thing, I'm convinced that we could cut the average 18-hole playing time by at least one hour.

THE POWER OF POSITIVE PUTTING

Successful putting—lining up the shot, sighting and finally stroking the ball—depends primarily on your attitude. Positive thinking on the greens can make a technically poor putter successful. Negative thinking —"If I miss this one, I'll never break 90 today"—will destroy good putting style because you cannot stroke a putt properly if anxiety has made you tense.

I suggest you try picturing the ball following a proper line into the hole. Do this when you sight the putt (see illustration) and then retain this image when you are over the ball, riveting your eyes to the back of the ball. Merely hit the ball along the line you have in your mind's eye.

It will take some practice to develop this power of visualization, but I guarantee that once you master the technique your putting will improve.

IMAGINATION IN PUTTING

The mind plays a major role in all phases of golf, but none requires a more positive mental outlook than does putting. Your mind, when properly used, can be a great aid toward success on the greens.

For instance, let's say you are having difficulty getting your long approach putts close enough for an easy sink. Chances are that you are trying to make these approach putts "too good." Tell yourself that you will settle for anything within 3 feet of the cup. Then imagine that the hole has suddenly expanded until it's 6

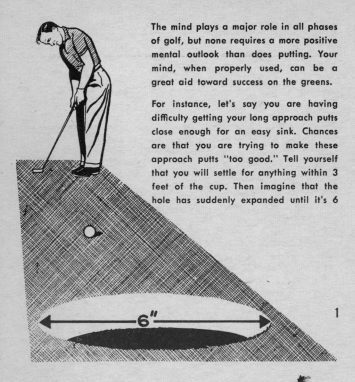

feet in diameter (as in illustration 1). Now all you have to do is stop your approach putt within this 6-foot area and you will be left with a second putt of less than 3 feet.

On short putts it helps to remember that the cup is actually more than 2½ times as wide as your ball's diameter (see illustration 2). There is plenty of room for those putts to drop.

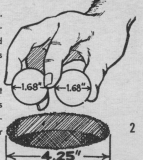

IMPROVE YOUR CHANCES FOR SINKING PUTTS

Don't let the diagrams here scare you. I'm not presenting an exercise in advanced geometry. However, I will show you how to increase the size of your putting target.

We've all heard the saying, "Never up, never in." Someone usually says it after you fall short on a putt. These diagrams will help me show why I disagree with this philosophy.

In illustration 1, we see the chances a player has when he banks away at the hole. Only when the ball squarely hits the back of the cup will it drop. In effect,

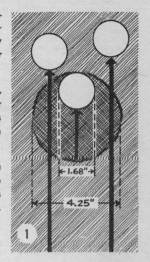

this player has reduced his hole from one of 4.25 inches in diameter to one no wider than the ball itself, or 1.68 inches.

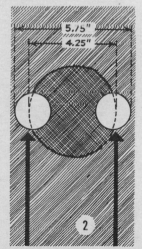

In illustration 2 we see the target for a golfer who hits his putts just the correct speed to reach the center of the hole. As putts that nick even the sides of the hole will drop if over one-half the ball hangs over the lip, it becomes apparent that the target is no longer merely 4.25 inches wide but rather about 5.75 inches in diameter.

Correct putting speed does widen your margin for error.

A KEY POINT ABOUT PUTTING

LIGHTLY HIT PUTT WILL TAKE MORE BREAK

HARDER HIT PUTT WILL GO STRAIGHTER

1

We all know that there are two ways to putt a ball on the sidehill. Either you can hit it relatively hard and allow for only a minimum of break, or you can stroke the ball gently and play for maximum break (illustration 1).

Now let's carry this knowledge a step further. Remember, we now know that a putt that is hit hard will take less break than one that is not.

2

AS BALL SLOWS DOWN IT BREAKS MORE AT END

BALL IS TRAVELLING WITH GREATER FORCE IN THE EARLY STAGES OF THE PUTT, CAUSING LESS BREAK

Suppose you have a sidehill putt of 10 feet and a similar putt from 20 feet. Would you allow for twice as much roll on the 20-footer because the ball must travel twice as far?

Of course not. As the 20-footer must be stroked harder, it will travel faster at first. Thus, it will be less susceptible to roll until it nears the hole (illustration 2).

This all may seem like mere common sense, but many golfers overlook the fact and allow for too much roll on long putts.

PLAYING FOR POSITION ON LONG PUTTS

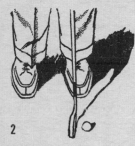

There is nothing shameful about playing conservatively on long putts, especially on contoured greens.

The golfer in illustration 1 has tried to sink a long one and has left himself a curling sidehiller.

If this same golfer had played his putt to finish below the cup, he would have been left with a fairly simple uphill tap-in (illustrations 2 and 3).

Of course, there will be times during a match when you must go for the cup on a long putt. However, under normal conditions the wise player will always consider beforehand from what position he would prefer to make his second putt if the first should miss the hole.

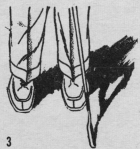

THERE ARE TIMES WHEN YOU SHOULD LAG PUTTS

Sidehill putting is an art. If the green is hard-packed or sun-baked or if the putt is fairly long (over 15 feet), I usually try to lag the ball to a distance just equal to the hole, and let the roll take it into the cup (see illustration 1).

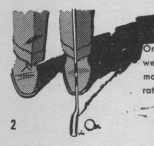

On shorter putts or when the green is wet and/or heavy, my follow-through is more abrupt as I hit for less roll. I'd rather "go for the cup."

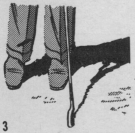

In illustration 3, my follow-through is abbreviated for the shorter sidehill putt, especially on a green in which Bermuda and rye grass predominate. Such grass slows the ball's progress. Rain, of course, will slow even the slickest of the Northern bent-grass greens.

LEARN FROM GOLFING MISTAKES

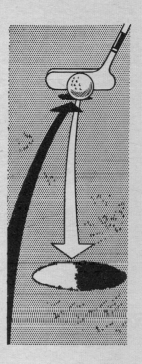

One of the best places to capitalize on your mistakes is on the putting green. Let's assume that you have just putted well past the hole, missing the cup on the left side.

The wise golfer will note the way the ball reacted as it rolled beyond the cup. He will note any curling of the ball to one side. Thus, he will be more knowledgeable about his return putt. He will know which way this second putt will break and approximately how much it will bend.

Avoid three-putt greens merely by noting closely the action of the ball on your first putt.

DON'T BABY THE RETURN PUTT

Many golfers who overshoot the hole on their first putt have a tendency to "baby" their return try.

If he has observed the break in his first putt, any golfer should have a pretty good idea how much break his second putt will take (see illustration).

With this knowledge, he should give the second putt a firm, smooth and accelerat-

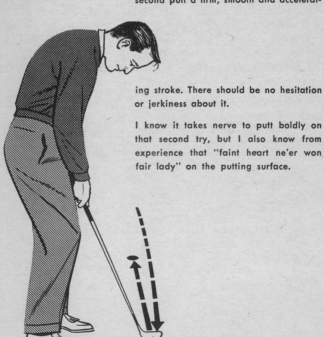

ing stroke. There should be no hesitation or jerkiness about it.

I know it takes nerve to putt boldly on that second try, but I also know from experience that "faint heart ne'er won fair lady" on the putting surface.

PUTTING GREEN'S TEXTURE DETERMINES AMOUNT OF "BREAK"

A factor that many golfers overlook, when trying to determine the line a putt will take, is the texture of the grass. Those golfers, who know that the texture affects the distance a putt will roll, fail to realize that it is also the texture which determines how much the putt will break.

As shown in the illustration, a putt will hold its line much better on a thick, "heavy" putting surface. When the grass is cut extremely short, you can count on the ball breaking when there is sidehill terrain.

The *variety* of the grass in question also affects the amount a putt will break to the side. Generally speaking, you can expect putts to take more break if the blades of grass are thin, and less break if they are thicker.

REGAINING YOUR PUTTING STROKE

Even the great putters, like Billy Casper, Bob Rosburg and Jerry Barber, occasionally have periods when their stroke seems out of kilter. Everyone, it seems, has a different method of gaining back their normal stroke. If you don't have such a method, here is one you might try.

First, try stroking putts for about 10 or 15 minutes, using only your right hand. Then, repeat the procedure using only

your left hand. Finally, put the two together and see if your stroke hasn't improved.

Putting with only one hand at a time forces a golfer to concentrate on stroking the ball squarely and to move the putter in a precise manner. In no time you will once again be giving every putt the best stroke you can.

CHAPTER 6

In and Out
of Trouble

•

Trouble is where you find it and it's not hard to find on a golf course. No player wants the stuff, of course; it just seems to seek him out.

Trouble on golf courses takes many forms—heavy grass, bushes, trees, boundaries, sand traps, ditches, streams, ponds, all the way up to rivers and oceans. Even the depression left when a preceding player gashed a divot from the fairway can become a premature grave for a golf ball.

The weather, too, often provides a measure of misery in the form of wind and rain, extremes of heat and cold.

Yet, it is the presence of these hazards that puts zest and challenge into the game. Without them, golf could be a downright bore. Can you imagine how unexciting it would be to play the game on a completely flat, unbroken carpet of grass one hole after another?

What some sportswriters have chosen to call "the magnetic appeal of Arnold Palmer" has developed in part from my occasional encounters with deep trouble during important tournament rounds. Average players identify with me in these tough spots. They seem to admire the risks I take, and the "determination" with which I attack the trouble shot.

Other players on the tour have just about as much ability but are perhaps too consistent, rarely straying from the straight and narrow. They have the respect and admiration of most golf fans, yet their perfection seems in a way to detract from their appeal.

This final chapter deals with virtually all of the forms of trouble a golfer might encounter on a course and explains how these problems should be handled. As sand traps are such a constant menace, considerable attention is given to the techniques of bunker play.

Several of the lessons deal with methods of playing holes to avoid trouble—such as when it makes sense to use something other than a driver off the tee or to play short of a green with less club rather than attempt to press a fairway wood to a green infested with trouble.

And, finally, this chapter offers cures for chronic shot problems that can put the player into the kind of trouble he must avoid if he is to become a respectable scorer.

SIMPLIFYING SAND SHOTS

These are the three sand-shot tips which cannot be stressed often enough.

(a) Once your footing is secure and firm, flex your knees more than would be necessary for a normal fairway shot (see illustration 1).

(b) Next, play the ball farther forward in your stance than usual (see illustration 2). You'll then have a better chance of striking the sand first, so that the club head can cut under the ball.

(c) Finally, imagine that you are slicing the sand with the left hand leading the club head from outside the target line (see illustration 3). An open stance will almost automatically insure this outside-in club-head path.

SAND STANCE

On normal bunker shots, all top-notch sand shooters use an open stance, in which the left foot is pulled back farther from the target line than is the right (see illustration 1).

1

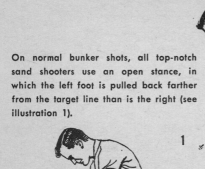

Such a stance helps your hip turn on the downswing; the left hip will be clear

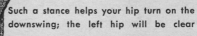

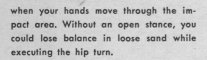

when your hands move through the impact area. Without an open stance, you could lose balance in loose sand while executing the hip turn.

Furthermore, the open stance allows you to pull your club head well to the inside during and after impact. Thus, you have a better chance of having the club head make a shallow cut and move through the sand more easily.

SAND TEXTURE AFFECTS TECHNIQUE

All too often, golfers hit shots from wet or hard sand in the same way they escape from bunkers filled with soft sand. The results are often disastrous.

First, it should be obvious that your club head will not cut so deeply into wet, hard or shallow sand—with mud just below the surface—as it will into soft, sifty sand.

You must note the texture of the sand and plan your shot accordingly.

When the sand is soft, try to penetrate it with your club head about 2 inches behind the ball. When the sand is firm, wet, or shallow, you should enter it closer to the ball, say about one to 1½ inches behind the ball.

As the firm sand will slow your club considerably, it is also very important not to quit on the shot. Give it a firm, full follow-through.

SOFT SAND

HARD SAND

THE SAND SHOT AND THE FIRM LEFT WRIST

The shallower the cut on a sand shot, the better. A deep cut would slow the club-head's progress through the ball.

Cutting too deeply is mostly caused by

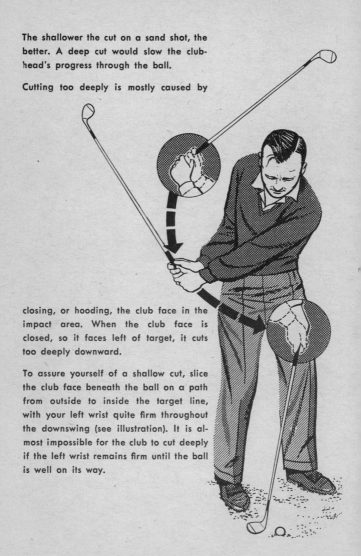

closing, or hooding, the club face in the impact area. When the club face is closed, so it faces left of target, it cuts too deeply downward.

To assure yourself of a shallow cut, slice the club face beneath the ball on a path from outside to inside the target line, with your left wrist quite firm throughout the downswing (see illustration). It is al-most impossible for the club to cut deeply if the left wrist remains firm until the ball is well on its way.

SAND SWING IS UPRIGHT

On normal sand shots the object is to contact the sand about an inch or two behind the ball (illustration 1) and to drive the club head under the ball so that the ball floats from the bunker on a cushion of sand.

Obviously, it would be disastrous if the club were to strike the ball before hitting the sand, or if the club were merely to graze the top of the sand. The ball would fly well past the target.

To eliminate these possibilities, your sand-shot swing should be more upright than for a normal fairway shot. Cocking your wrists early on the backswing (see illustration 2) will help your swing achieve an upright character (illustration 3). This upright swing will give you the club-head path needed to cut under the ball and through the sand.

SAND-TRAP POINTERS

As far as sand shots are concerned, the deeper the ball rests in the sand, the deeper your club must cut into the bunker. And the less loft you allow your club to assume, the deeper it will cut into the sand.

Therefore, less loft is best for buried lies; additional loft is best when the ball sits atop the sand.

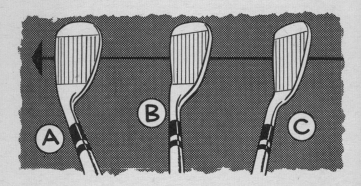

The amount of loft your club assumes is determined by the position of your hands. If you wish a club to assume more loft than normal, you address the shot with your hands behind the ball. If you wish less loft, merely position your hands farther forward, well ahead of the ball.

THE SLOW-MOTION APPROACH TO SAND SHOOTING

Too many golfers are too anxious to get sand shots out of the way, so they unconsciously increase their swing tempo and fail to make the shots as planned.

Why not try practicing sand shots in slow motion? It will help a lot.

Then try to duplicate this rhythm in actual play. Focus your attention on a spot behind the ball and swing slowly and firmly.

A side benefit also accrues from a slow sand-shot swing. By swinging slowly, the golfer will minimize chances that his feet will slip in the sand, as they might on a faster swing.

A "HERO SHOT" FROM SAND

Don't despair when your ball finishes near the high lip of a sand bunker, as shown in illustration 1. Your fellow players will be expecting the worst. It's your chance to make a real "hero shot."

Obviously, the problem is to make the ball rise very quickly, almost straight up. Here's how we'll do it:

First, play the ball well forward in your stance, even ahead of your front foot. By playing it from this position with a wedge or 9-iron, you will find that the club almost lays on its backside, thus providing the necessary loft.

Next, position your feet so that your forward foot is pulled well back from the target line (illustration 1). Make sure that the club face, however, still faces the target.

Finally, swing into the ball from outside to inside the target line so that the club head moves along a path parallel to the position of your feet (illustration 2). Contact the sand about an inch behind the ball and it will pop up and over the bunker's lip.

HOW TO PLAY DOWNHILL SAND SHOTS

The biggest problem on downhill sand shots is the possibility that the club head might cut into the side of the ball, instead of beneath it.

On such shots, concentrate on contacting the sand well behind the ball and sliding your club head through the sand, well beyond the ball's original position (see illustration 1).

To make such a cut through the sand, I advise a slight change in the positioning of your shoulders at address.

On all normal shots, your right shoulder should be slightly lower than your left (illustration 2) because your right hand Is lower than your left on the club shaft.

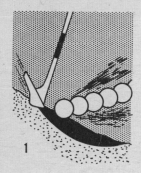

However, on downhill sand shots, position your right shoulder a bit higher than your left (illustration 3). This will assure you of an upright swing and will cause you to take a healthy cut of sand so as to sclaff or top the shot.

PLAY BALL BACK ON UPHILL SAND SHOTS

UPHILL **NORMAL**

The big danger on uphill sand shots is that the club head will not get through all the sand in front of the ball. Even if it does get through, the loss of club-head speed may cause the ball to fall short.

Thus, it is important that on such shots your club head enter the sand close to the ball, instead of an inch or two behind it as it normally would.

Play normal sand shots as I do—off the left heel (see dotted-line drawing)—and cut in well behind the ball. On uphill sand shots, however, play the ball farther back in your stance (note solid-line drawing). This will cause your club head to enter the sand closer to the ball so that little club-head speed will be lost before the ball is on its way.

TWO ALTERNATIVES OUT OF SAND

Under most circumstances, it is best to use the sand wedge from any trap. However, other clubs can be used to escape sand.

For instance, if there is no lip on the greenside of the trap, and the cub is close to the near edge of the green, a putter can be used. Play the ball in the center of your stance and hit it hard enough so it will fly until it hits solid ground.

When the sand is extremely hard, as after a rain, the ball may be chipped out. Again, there should be no lip between you and the green, as the ball won't pop up when a chipping iron is used and might be stopped by this raised portion of ground.

Play the ball back toward the right foot and make sure the club head strikes the ball before the sand—much like a regular chip.

PITCHING WEDGE BEST FOR BURIED LIES

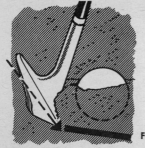

1

For hitting a shot from a buried lie, you must use a club with a heavyweight head and sharp, leading edge. That's why a pitching wedge is tailor-made for such shots. If you don't own a pitching wedge, the 9-iron would be your next choice.

Plan to hit such a shot just as you would a normal fairway-wedge shot, except see that the club enters the sand behind the ball (illustration 1). If you retain your weight on your left foot and cock your wrists quickly on your backswing, you will get the sharply descending downswing you need to cut well under the ball.

Above all, remember to swing well through on the shot with a firm left-hand grip (illustration 2).

2

LONG SHOTS FROM SAND

Long shots from sand seem to cause the average golfer lots of trouble. I think the problem in most cases is simply that the player doesn't know how to execute this shot. It really isn't difficult at all.

All you must do is contact the ball before your club enters the sand (see illustration

1). Here is how you make sure this happens:

First, settle your feet in the sand so that they won't shift during the swing.

Play the ball from the same position in your stance that you would use on a normal fairway shot with a club at hand.

Emphasize placing most of your weight on your left foot at address.

Swing largely with your arms, keeping your weight on your left foot, as you see me doing in illustration 2.

Meet the ball just before your club head enters the sand (illustration 3).

As you will note, everything I have mentioned is designed to keep body movement to a minimum so that your club will meet the ball before hitting the sand.

HOW TO HIT AN IRON SHOT UNDER TROUBLE

A fairly common trouble shot is one where the golfer must punch an iron shot on a low trajectory so that it passes under the leaves of a tree.

I prefer to play this shot well back in my stance, as in illustration 1, with my hands well forward. This decreases the effective loft on the club and encourages my striking the ball on my downswing.

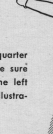

I seldom take more than a three-quarter backswing on this shot and I make sure that my weight shifts quickly to the left very early on my downswing (illustration 2).

As I am striking the ball while my club is still moving downward, I must be careful that I do not lift my head and shoulders. If I don't "stay down" with this shot, the club might merely pass across the top of the ball instead of contacting it solidly.

Because I stress keeping my head down, I seldom finish the swing with my hands much higher than my shoulders (illustration 3).

PLAY IT SQUARE IN THE ROUGH

In shooting from the rough, try to get out in one shot. An absolutely square hit is essential.

Use a wood only from light rough, and play the ball well forward.

An iron shot from medium rough (illustrated) which is likely to reach the green, should cause the golfer to remember this: Such a shot will have little backspin, so land the ball in front of the green, if you have an opening, and let the ball run on.

The wedge is often the only way out of deep rough. Keep the club face square at all times.

If the ball is setting up, get the feeling you're going to cut the grass out from under the ball. The ball will probably fly high, certainly an advantage if there are trees to clear.

If the ball is snuggled down, hit it before hitting the grass—and crisply.

AN EASY WAY TO MAKE SHOTS
FROM ROUGH

When hitting shots out of rough, your
sole concern should be to contact the ball
squarely with a minimum of interference
from the surrounding grass.

You will want your club head to enter
the hitting area on a sharply descending
path so that it will move into the ball
relatively uninhibited.

One way to assure yourself of such a
club-head path is to cock your wrists
earlier than normal on the backswing and
to retain most of your weight on your left
foot (see illustration).

This sort of swing will also decrease your
body turn and thus aid in making square
contact with the ball.

"EXPLODE" SHORT SHOTS FROM THE ROUGH

I'm sure that all golfers can recall times when they have hit behind the ball unintentionally. They will recall how the ball sort of floated through the air and then fell short of the target.

This same shot can be made intentionally to good advantage. It should be used when you find yourself near the green with the ball lying low in deep grass.

Play this shot just as you would an explosion shot from sand. Play the ball forward in your stance as you would on a sand shot (illustration 1) and then swing so that the club head enters the turf behind the ball (illustration 2).

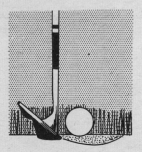

The best club for this shot is a pitching wedge or a 9-iron. Such a club will float the ball out of the rough and onto the green so that it will settle quickly.

APPROACH SHOTS CALL FOR PREPLANNING

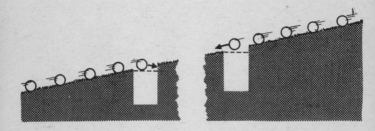

This illustration clearly shows why you should play approach shots to finish below the hole, so that you leave yourself an uphill putt.

The ball which runs uphill to the hole has the higher edge of the hole acting as a built-in backstop. The downhill putt, on the other hand, has little or no backstop. A putt stuck too hard downhill has less of a chance of sinking in than an uphill putt has.

Also, remember that an uphill putt will stop closer to the hole if it misses the cup than will a downhill putt, which gravity causes to roll on and on.

USE UPRIGHT SWING WHEN BALL IS BURIED

When you find that your ball lies in a depression, such as an old divot mark (see illustration 1), don't panic. Unless the ball is deeply buried, you should be able to execute an iron shot that will bring practically the same result you'd get from a normal lie.

To dislodge the ball from a depressed lie, your club head must be descending sharply as it comes into the ball (note solid line in illustration 2). If the club head is not descending sharply (dotted line), it may strike the turf behind the ball or catch only the top part of the ball.

You will achieve the upright swing if you retain more weight than normal on your left foot throughout your swing, especially during your backswing. The weight distribution to your left causes your club head to rise quickly on the backswing and descend sharply on the downswing.

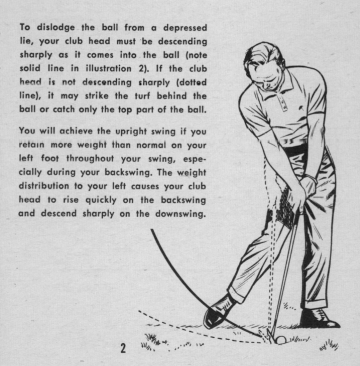

A TIME TO PLAY SAFE

I seldom advocate playing "safe" in a golf tournament. Too often, playing safe when you are ahead turns your game into a defensive one. Pretty soon, you are thinking negatively and then you lose your lead.

However, there is one occasion in match play when every golfer should play it safe. That situation occurs when your opponent's shot flies out of bounds.

When this occurs, he has, in effect, handed you two free shots. Don't waste them.

If your opponent's drive has gone out of bounds, you should tee off with the club you can be sure will keep you in the fairway, even if it may be an iron (see illustration).

It may not seem sporting to resort to these tactics, but there is really nothing questionable about doing so. It's just smart strategy.

IF YOUR
OPPONENT S BALL
IS OUT OF BOUNDS
FROM THE TEE,
PLAY IT SAFE AND
USE AN IRON.

PICK THE BALL CLEANLY FROM WET TURF

In hitting iron shots from firm, dry turf, most good golfers take a divot just after contacting the ball (see illustration 1).

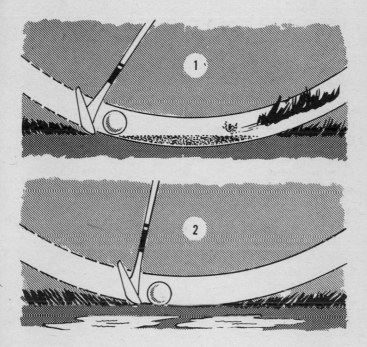

But from wet, soggy turf, they pick the ball cleanly. The club head doesn't cut deeply and the ball isn't pinched against wet turf, thus causing the shot to fall short of its normal range.

To follow their example and pick cleanly, play the ball a bit farther forward than normal, more toward the target (see illustration 2). By doing this, you can see you will strike the ball at the bottom of your swing instead of slightly higher on the downstroke. Just be sure you don't cut into the turf behind the ball.

USE A TEE WHEN PLAYING THE PAR-3

Some amateur golfers simply toss aside an advantage given them by the rules when they fail to hit iron tee shots on par-3 holes off a wooden tee. Some of these players just set the ball down and hit the shot as they would off the fairway. Others nudge it up on a tuft of grass, thus eliminating their chances of applying maximum back-spin to the ball.

I suggest you play such shots from a low-setting tee. In effect, this places the ball almost level with the ground, yet puts it on a firmer surface than even the ground itself. Teeing the ball in this manner will allow you to apply plenty of backspin to the ball. And even a slightly mis-hit shot from a tee will produce better results than it would off the turf.

NEVER MISJUDGE DISTANCE FACTOR

A shot from an elevated tee or fairway to a green below will travel farther than will a shot to a green on the same level. The illustration shows why this is so. Note that the ball travels farther because of its extended parabola.

By the same token, if you shoot to a raised green, you can expect that the ball will not travel so far as normally.

Normally, my shots will travel about 10 feet farther if the hitting area is 20 feet higher than the green. The reverse applies to elevated greens.

This knowledge should prove helpful, especially on par-3 holes, so many of which include elevated tees or greens. Also, par-3 holes are often well-guarded by hazards or rough. Misjudgment of distance can be especially harmful.

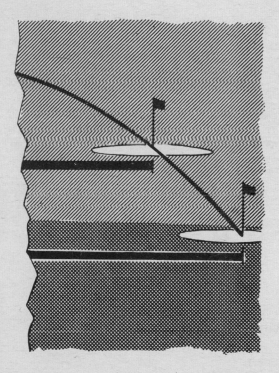

SHOOTING FROM A DIVOT MARK

When you find yourself facing a shot out of a divot mark, remember to let the club head strike the ball before it contacts the turf. In this way, dirt between the club face and the ball won't spoil the shot.

1

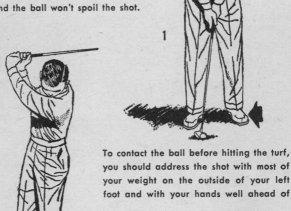

2

3

To contact the ball before hitting the turf, you should address the shot with most of your weight on the outside of your left foot and with your hands well ahead of the ball (illustration 1). By keeping most of your weight on the left foot throughout the swing, you will find that your club head will raise and then lower to the ball on a sharply descending angle (illustration 2).

This abrupt angle of descent will let your club head miss the back edge of the divot hole and strike the ball solidly (illustration 3).

PIN POSITION AFFECTS CLUB SELECTION

In this era of 10,000-square foot greens, it has become even more important to check pin position before selecting your approaching club.

When the green runs 90—100 feet from front to back, you may have a choice of 3 different clubs, 2 of which would leave your shot either short or long (see illustration).

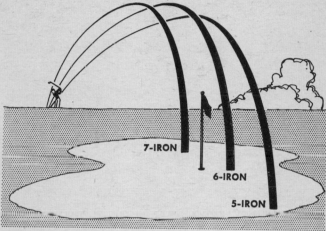

7-IRON
6-IRON
5-IRON

There probably are some holes on your course that do not allow a good view of the green from the fairway. Try to note the pin position on these greens as you play other holes earlier in the round. I always check the pin position on the 18th green at the Masters tournament as I walk from the 9th green to the 10th tee.

If you are in doubt about the club selection, note where the trouble lies around the green; is it in front or behind the green? Then select a club which will keep you out of the worst trouble.

WHEN TO TAKE THE OFFENSE;
WHEN TO "PLAY FOR PAR"

I may be regarded as an "attacking" golfer, but I am also cautious if the odds for a successful shot aren't a lot better than 50—50.

The Augusta National course, where the Masters is played yearly, is dotted with "attacking" and "defensive" holes.

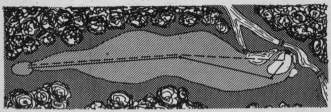

1

The 11th there, for example, definitely calls for conservatism (see illustration 1). A second shot, hit for the pin, may wind up in the water which guards the green on the left and in front. On this hole, I prefer to play my second shot to the right, hoping to chip or long-putt close enough for a par.

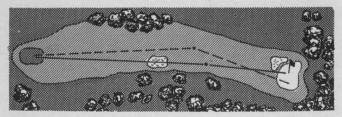

2

The first hole at Augusta, on the other hand (illustration 2), calls for an offensive tee shot. Here I like to play over that right-side bunker you see there. Such a shot shortens the hole and opens the green for a fairly easy approach and a possible birdie.

SOUND STRATEGY TO SAVE STROKES

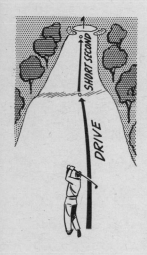

Golf-course architects seem to be relying more and more on sand bunkers around greens to test a golfer's skill. Often we find only a very narrow opening to the putting surface.

Still, golfers continue to try to shoot through these narrow avenues. This can be a costly practice, especially for players who are a bit shaky on sand shots.

I advise most golfers to play short of such greens (see illustration) unless they are reasonably certain that they can carry the bunkers.

If you play short, you will still be in good position to pitch onto the green and one-putt. You can still get a par on par-4 holes and, possibly, a birdie on short par-5's.

You will be reasonably sure of having a good lie in the fairway from which to play your next shot. If you go for the green and hit the sand, you might come up with a bad lie and ruin your round by going several over par.

PLAN WHERE MISSED SHOTS WILL FINISH

Though I really hate to inject negative thinking into golf, sometimes it pays to be realistic. The truth is that even a great golfer can't honestly expect to hit more than a few very good shots during a round of play.

The golfer should develop the type of thinking that allows a pool player to plan future shots in advance. Every time you step up to a full shot, you should determine where you want your ball to finish if you should miss the shot.

In the illustration, we see a golfer hitting down the fairway. Let's assume that you are this golfer and that you have a tendency to slice shots.

If you are wise, you will aim to the left side of the fairway (solid line). Even if the ball slices, you will still have a shot to the green. However, if you aim for the pin and slice (dotted line), you will be in trouble.

Realize your shot-making weakness and minimize its adverse effect by looking ahead for best position for your next shot.

PLAYING IT SMART

In the illustration, we see a situation that faces every golfer sooner or later. The drive has caught the fairway rough, and the player faces a shot of about 190 yards to a green guarded by sand traps.

The golfer must decide whether to hit an iron from the rough, playing short of the hazards, or to try a wood shot, hoping to reach the green so that he can two-putt for a par.

Unless the player MUST win or birdie this hole to stay in contention, I think he should resist the temptation to reach the green in 2 with the wood club. If he doesn't meet the ball solidly, or if he doesn't fly it straight to the flag, he will face either a long third shot to the green from the fairway, or a short one from the sand trap. In either case, his chances for a par will be quite slim.

On the other hand, if he plays the relatively safe iron shot from the rough—predetermining where he wants the shot to finish—he will leave only a short pitch shot to the green. He will still have a relatively good chance for his par, with little danger of a double-bogey.

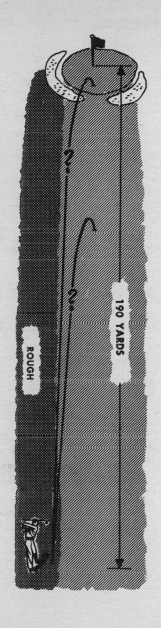

ROUGH

190 YARDS

PLAN YOUR ROUND AND LOWER YOUR SCORE

If you shoot about 90 for an average round of golf, clear-think your way into the low 80s—occasionally the high 70s.

First, plan your round. Chances are that now you get about 6 pars in 18 holes. You propably get about 7 bogies, 4 double-bogies and maybe 1 disastrous quadruple-bogey.

Analyze what's needed to lower your score from 90 to 80. All you must do is to par one more hole. You can do that. Also change those double-bogies to bogies and eliminate the bad hole.

If you are good enough to shoot 90, you are good enough to eliminate double-bogies, for the most part. Just think clearly on each hole and make up your mind that you won't go more than one over par. Here's what I mean:

The hole is 430 yards, par 4. Probably you cannot reach it in two shots. Don't try. Just keep the ball in play. Two straight shots and you'll be about 30 yards short of the green (see illustration). All you must do then is hit the ball somewhere on the green and two-putt for your bogey. You might even approach for one putt and a par.

Just keep the ball in play and the bad hole and double-bogies will vanish.

2 WOOD
190 YDS.

DRIVE
210 YDS.

SAFE WAY IS BEST WAY ON THIS SHORT SHOT

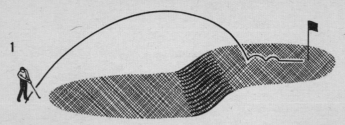

When golfers encounter a short shot to a 2-level green, deciding which club to use might be tough.

The player may elect to swing a highly lofted club and pitch the shot to the upper level (illustration 1).

Or he may choose a less lofted club and play the shot short of the incline (illustration 2).

The golfer should play the shot in which he has the most confidence. However, I would like to point out one thing.

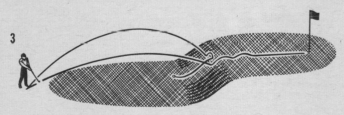

You will note in illustration 3 what happens when the player misjudges the shot and the ball hits into the incline. See how the highly lofted shot fails to make the grade while the lower run-up shot still scoots up to the hole.

This makes the run-up shot best under such circumstance, in my opinion.

THE "FENCE" SHOT

1

Most golf courses today have fences of some sort along their borders. If your ball comes to rest near a fence, the rules require you to play it or take an unplayable lie penalty. You will save yourself strokes if you know how to play such shots.

The problem is less difficult if the fence is on the opposite side of the ball from where you must stand. In such instances, merely turn the club face inward (illustration 1) and swing backward and forward on a line parallel to the fence so that your club head will not catch in the fence (illustration 2). Because of the closed club face, your ball will fly forward, but away from the fence into safe territory.

2

3

If you must stand on the fence side of the ball, it helps to be slightly ambidextrous. Here you must invert the club as I have in illustration 3 and swing left-handed. Again the angle of the club face will automatically cause it to fly away from the fence. You will be a real hero among your golf buddies if you practice the fence shot until you have it perfected and can pull it off during play.

AIMING SHOTS IN A CROSSWIND

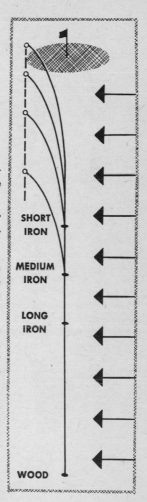

The average golfer figures that a crosswind will have more effect on his tee shots than on a short-iron approach.

"The drive travels farther in the wind," he says, "so I have to allow more for wind drag on the shot."

This is not necessarily true. All things being equal, a given crosswind will have no more or no less effect on a drive than it will on a wedge shot.

True, the drive stays in the air for a longer time and for a greater distance, but it also travels with greater velocity and therefore is better able to resist the crosswind effect.

Remember this the next time you play a crosswind shot. Try allowing for less wind effect on a long shot and for more on a short shot.

Also, when playing in a crosswind, it's usually best merely to allow for the wind's effect when you aim. Don't try to cut or draw shots into the wind. The more shots you can hit with your normal swing, the better you will score.

DON'T PRESS FOR EXTRA YARDAGE INTO STRONG WIND

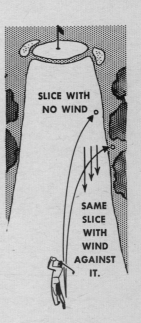

SLICE WITH NO WIND

SAME SLICE WITH WIND AGAINST IT.

Shots into the wind that carry any amount of sidespin will be pushed off-line to a greater degree than would be normal on a still day (see illustration). They not only fly farther off-line, but they also fly much shorter than normal because of the wind.

The next time you play a shot into the wind, forget about distance. Just give the shot your best swing, one that will strike the ball as squarely as possible. Stress control, rather than length. By striking the ball squarely—even if it means shortening your swing—you not only will achieve a shot of decent length, but, more important, you will keep the ball in play.

INTO WIND USE MORE CLUB AND LESS SWING

When you must hit iron shots into the wind, you need a low-flying, well-controlled ball flight. You want the ball to fly low, so it will be less affected by the wind than if it flew high. You want the shot to be well-controlled because a headwind tends to increase any sidespin on the ball, thus accentuating a hook or a slice.

You can achieve a low-flying shot by using a less lofted club than normal. Also, you will get less height if you play the ball a bit farther back than normal in your stance. Since a less lofted club, say a 4-iron, will fly farther than a more lofted club, say a 6-iron, you must shorten your swing slightly when using the less lofted club. The shorter swing also gives you the better control you need in the wind.

I'm shown swinging a normal 4-iron in illustration 1. Note how much shorter my swing is in illustration 2, where I'm still swinging a 4-iron, but in the manner I'd use for a headwind.

AVOID SWING CHANGES WHENEVER POSSIBLE

On crosswind shots either you can aim to the left or right and let the wind bring in the shot, or you can alter your swing to fade or draw the shot into the force of the wind. I much prefer the former option as it involves no swing changes.

Merely select an object to the side of the pin from which the wind is blowing and hit the shot toward this object. Obviously, the force of the wind will determine how much you must alter your aim.

When playing in the wind, it is also wise to look at treetops to determine the force of the wind at that height. Often a slight breeze at ground level may be of much stronger force higher up where your ball will be traveling.

A FINER POINT OF PLAY

I am abandoning you weekend golfers for the moment and aiming my advice at golfers who really want to excel at the game.

A straight shot is most difficult to produce and is, therefore, an undependable goal. Highly successful golfers prefer to develop a swing pattern that produces a slight bend to their normal shots. A left-to-right or right-to-left shot, they find, can be more consistently executed.
If you ever aim to shoot par or better, work with your local pro to devlop such a shot pattern.

If you are now a long hitter, you will find the left-to-right shot pattern (for right-handers) the best for accuracy. Shorter hitters may need the added distance one gets from right-to-left shots, which usually produce more roll.

FADING THE APPROACH

Put most of the weight on the left foot at address and do not shift much as you swing the club back. Aim for a three-quarters swing and break the wrists a bit earlier on the backswing. Let the left knee bend toward the ball as you swing back. Get the hands high at the finish.

When greens are especially fast, steps should be taken to keep iron approaches from running off the putting surface. A great shot to a hard green is a fade, where the ball curves slightly from left to right and comes down easily. Use an open stance, as illustrated.

A VALUABLE SHOT TO MASTER

The back-climbing shot can save you valuable strokes, And it really is not a difficult shot to execute.

This shot should be used when you are shooting to a raised green and when the pin is positioned so near your side of the green that you cannot possibly pitch the ball onto the green and expect it to stop in time.

Instead, you select a low lofted club, such as a 2-iron, and run the ball up the bank.

The key to this shot is to hit it so that it makes a series of short, low bounces rather than only a few large bounces. The latter, too often, bounce into the side of the hill and die.

Play these shots well back in your stance, even to the right of stance-center, so that you can strike with a crisp downward blow straight through the ball. You will be tempted to lift your head on this shot, so keep your eyes steady on the back of the ball.

SIDEHILL SIDEWINDERS

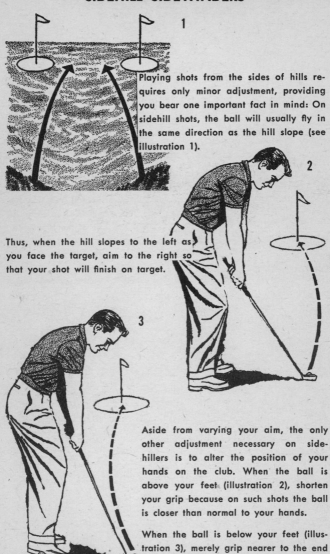

1

Playing shots from the sides of hills requires only minor adjustment, providing you bear one important fact in mind: On sidehill shots, the ball will usually fly in the same direction as the hill slope (see illustration 1).

2

Thus, when the hill slopes to the left as you face the target, aim to the right so that your shot will finish on target.

3

Aside from varying your aim, the only other adjustment necessary on sidehillers is to alter the position of your hands on the club. When the ball is above your feet (illustration 2), shorten your grip because on such shots the ball is closer than normal to your hands.

When the ball is below your feet (illustration 3), merely grip nearer to the end of the club.

HOW TO HIT STRAIGHT SHOTS FROM HILLY LIES

Most golfers have trouble hitting straight shots from uphill or downhill lies. Because the player's weight shifts so readily to his lower side, the path of the club head is thrown out of kilter.

Normally, a golfer will push shots to the right from a downhill lie and pull them to the left from an uphill lie.

To counteract this tendency, the golfer should consciously put more weight on his higher foot at address (see illustrations). Try to keep much of your weight on the higher foot throughout your swing. Straighter shots should result.

UPHILL LIES SHOULDN'T PRESENT PROBLEMS

To tackle uphill lies, remember these tips:

1. Play the ball more forward than usual (see illustration 1).

2. Keep the ball from flying high and pulling to the left by selecting a club with less loft than normal for the desired distance.

3. Bend your "uphill" knee to keep hips level and aim to right of target.

4. Maintain a long and low backswing (see illustration 2), but don't shift too much weight to the right.

The slant may make it difficult to get your weight back to the left on the downswing.

5. As with downhill lies, let the club head follow the ground's contour.

6. Don't let the wrists turn over too soon after impact, and stay down on the ball.

TIPS FOR DOWNHILL LIES

On downhill lies, play the ball toward the right foot. Level the hips by bending the right (or rear) leg. Aim to left of target, as the tendency is to push or fade on this type of shot.

Once you learn to stay "down" on the ball after impact, downhill shots will come easier. This is part of the maxim that the swing must follow the contour of the ground—thus the club head should be especially low for as long as possible after the ball is struck.

THE HANDY "PUNCH" SHOT

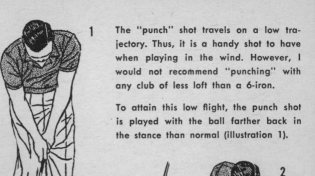

1

The "punch" shot travels on a low trajectory. Thus, it is a handy shot to have when playing in the wind. However, I would not recommend "punching" with any club of less loft than a 6-iron.

To attain this low flight, the punch shot is played with the ball farther back in the stance than normal (illustration 1).

2

3

The backswing should be short and compact, with most of the weight remaining on the left foot throughout (illustration 2).

Because the ball is played back, it will be struck on the downswing, before the club meets the turf. The club head will take a sizable divot well ahead of the original ball position. Obviously, a tight grip and a firm left arm are necessary.

LEARNING THE "CUT" SHOT

If you don't own a sand wedge and if the greens at your club are usually hard, learn the "cut" shot. Even if you are using a 9-iron or a pitching wedge, the "cut" moves the club head through the sand readily and doesn't allow it to cut too deeply. From the fairway, the cut shot pitches the ball high into the air with a lot of backspin, so it settles quickly on hard greens.

Here, I illustrate the things to do to produce a cut shot. Play the ball forward, opposite the left heel. Use the open stance. Let the left hand remain firm on the downswing and don't let the club face close at impact. If anything, the club face should be facing to the right of target on this shot.

THE INTENTIONAL SLICE

1 Successfully executing intentionally sliced or hooked shots can make you look like an expert in your golfing companions' eyes. However, these shots should be practiced or you might look very foolish.

There are three things you can do to slice intentionally. First, you can weaken your

2

grip by turning your hands more to the left on the club (illustration 1).

Second, you can address the ball in an open-stance position, with your left foot pulled farther back than your right from

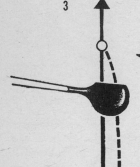

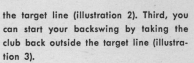

3

the target line (illustration 2). Third, you can start your backswing by taking the club back outside the target line (illustration 3).

The degree your ball slices will be determined by the number of these techniques you use and the amount in each case you depart from what is normal for you. The best procedure is usually the open stance, keeping the rest of your swing as usual.

THE INTENTIONAL HOOK

1

There comes a time in every golfer's life when he needs the ability to produce an intentionally hooked shot. If you practice the following hook-producing techniques, you will be ready to handle any such situation!

First, strengthen your grip by turning your hands farther to the right than normal on the club (illustration 1).

3

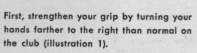

2

Second, close your stance by placing your right foot farther than your left from the line to the target (illustration 2). Third, on your backswing, take the club head back well inside the target line (illustration 3).

Again, as in the sliced shot, a change in stance is usually sufficient.

CURING THE PUSH

Incorrect body action, which causes the club face to be open at impact, usually results in a push. These are shots which fly straight, but to the right,

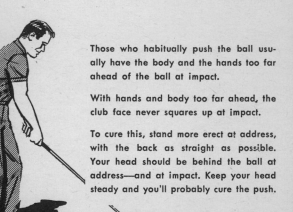

Those who habitually push the ball usually have the body and the hands too far ahead of the ball at impact.

With hands and body too far ahead, the club face never squares up at impact.

To cure this, stand more erect at address, with the back as straight as possible. Your head should be behind the ball at address—and at impact. Keep your head steady and you'll probably cure the push.

PROTECTING AGAINST THE HOOK

Golfers whose shots either fly straight to the left (pull) or fly and bend to the left (sharp hook) should check their shoulder action on the downswing.

If the shoulders turn on too level a plane (illustration 1), the club may move into the hitting area from outside the target line. Normally, this will drive the ball to the left.

A simple solution to this problem is to work the shoulders on more of an up-down pattern on the downswing. Concentrate on either lowering your right shoulder or raising your left (illustration 2) as you move into the hitting area.

This proper shoulder action will keep the club head moving well inside the target line on the downswing and along the target line in the hitting area. The club face will drive the ball forward, instead of to the left.

HOOKING REMEDIES

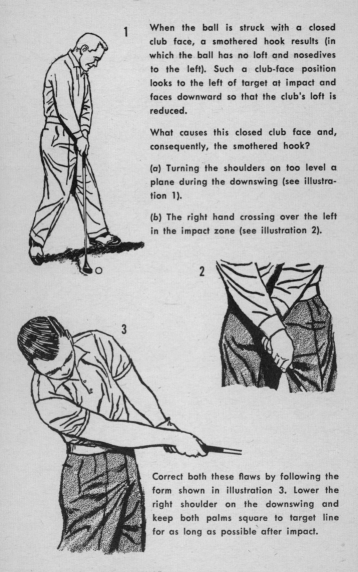

1

When the ball is struck with a closed club face, a smothered hook results (in which the ball has no loft and nosedives to the left). Such a club-face position looks to the left of target at impact and faces downward so that the club's loft is reduced.

What causes this closed club face and, consequently, the smothered hook?

(a) Turning the shoulders on too level a plane during the downswing (see illustration 1).

(b) The right hand crossing over the left in the impact zone (see illustration 2).

2

3

Correct both these flaws by following the form shown in illustration 3. Lower the right shoulder on the downswing and keep both palms square to target line for as long as possible after impact.

THE "WHY" OF SKIED SHOTS

The most common reason for a skied shot —one that flies up, but with little distance—is a dropped right shoulder after impact. Golfers mistakenly think they're going to get more power into the shot. What happens is that the swing arc is incorrectly lowered.

If you're having trouble with these skied shots, or if you're hitting behind the ball too often, concentrate on a smooth downswing. Don't let the right hand, arm or shoulder take over all the power. The left side should lead the club head into and through the ball.

"FAT" SHOT CURES

Ever get into a streak of hitting "fat" shots, those in which the club head hits behind the ball? You lose distance; the ball loses direction.

One cause is a crouched stance. In other words, the player bends his knees too much at address. His arms will also usually bend. Then, when he swings, he straightens his arms—and another "fat" shot results.

Stand straighter if you're having this trouble. Your arms should hang naturally from your shoulders, and should not be bent.

Besides curing "fat" shot tendencies, this stance will give you a wider swing arc and more power.

SLICERS—BEWARE OF OPEN STANCE

A familiar sight on almost any golf course is the player who compensates for his slice by aiming to the left side of the fairway. He pulls his left foot back from the target line, thus providing himself with an "open" stance (illustration 1).

This is merely a compensation—not a cure—for slicing. The player still gets a "banana ball" and the loss of distance that goes with such a shot.

Actually, this player encourages a slice by aiming to the left. His open stance encourages an outside-in club-head path (illustration 2) which puts a slice spin (clockwise) on the ball.

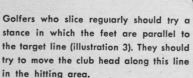

Golfers who slice regularly should try a stance in which the feet are parallel to the target line (illustration 3). They should try to move the club head along this line in the hitting area.

Try this on a few shots. It may cure your slice. If it doesn't, see your pro for more detailed instruction.

TOPPING CAN BE ELIMINATED; HERE'S HOW

1

Improper positioning of club head and ball at address can result in topped shots, among other things. (A topped shot is one in which you contact the ball above its center.)

2

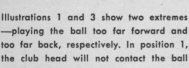

Illustrations 1 and 3 show two extremes —playing the ball too far forward and too far back, respectively. In position 1, the club head will not contact the ball

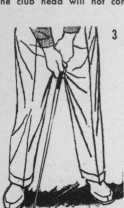

3

until it has started its upswing. In position 3, the club head will hit the ball before it reaches the bottom of the downswing.

Strike the happy medium, as shown in illustration 2. Play the ball about opposite the left heel for drives. As you progress to shorter clubs, the ball position moves farther back in the stance.

3 CAUSES OF TOPPED SHOTS

A common cause of topped shots is the tendency to bend too much from the knees at address (illustration 1). You might think that bending your knees would lessen your chances of hitting the ball on top. But, unfortunately, the person who crouches at address has a tendency to straighten his knees during the swing. Naturally this raises the hands and the club so that it passes over the top of the ball.

The club head also rises and tops shots if your right elbow flies away from your side on the downswing (illustration 2) or if your left elbow bends on the downswing (illustration 3).

If you top shots, try (a) "feeling tall" when addressing the ball, (b) bringing your right elbow to the side on the downswing, or (c) maintaining an extended left arm through impact.

Above all, let your club's loft provide height for the shot. Never feel that you must scoop the ball into the air. Sweep the ball with the woods and pinch it against the turf with a slightly downward blow on iron shots.

CURE FOR PULLED SHOTS

1

The pulled shot differs from the push in that it flies to the left rather than to the right. It differs from the hook in that it flies on a straight line rather than in a bending curve. The pull occurs when the club, facing left, moves into the hitting area from outside the target line.

2

One major cause of the pulled shot is lazy footwork (illustration 1). Here, the player has swung flatfooted and failed to transfer his weight to the left on the downswing. The resulting roundhouse swing sends the ball to the left.

3

For proper footwork, roll to the instep of your left foot on the backswing, lifting the heel slightly, as you see me doing in illustration 2. Then immediately return the left heel to the ground and let the right foot roll gradually to its instep on the downswing (illustration 3).

MORE ON PULLED SHOTS

1

If you are bothered by pulled shots, which fly on a straight line, but to the left of target, your problem may lie in the way you turn your shoulders on your downswing.

When a golfer fails to lower his right shoulder sufficiently on his downswing (illustration 1), his club enters the hitting area from outside the target line (illus-

tration 2). If the club face is facing to the left, the shot will fly in that direction. If it's facing at the target the ball will slice to the right.

To avoid such off-line shots, you must keep your club head inside the target line. Return your right elbow to your right side and lower your right shoulder early in your downswing (illustration 3) and your club head will enter the hitting area from inside the line (illustration 4). Straighter shots will result.

A CURE FOR THE "SHANKS"

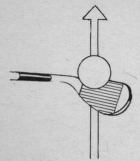

When you hit your iron shots on the hosel of the club (illustration 1) and they shoot off to the right, you are a victim of "shanked" shots. Shanked shots are bad enough in themselves, but even worse when the shanks lead to the "shakes."

1

2

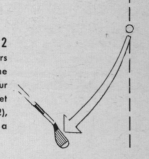

There are several reasons that golfers shank shots, but a very common one occurs on the backswing. If you take your club back too much "inside" the target line, around your body (illustration 2), you will be likely to return it along a

path that forces the club head "outside" the ball (illustration 3). The result will be that the club's shaft, instead of its face, strikes the ball.

3

4

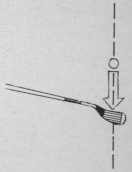

If you shank shots, I suggest you try taking the club back more along the target line—straighter back from the ball (illustration 4). This will encourage your returning the club face squarely into the ball.

CONCLUSION

Now that you have read through the book, don't let it go at that. Read it again and again, trying out the grip with an actual club, taking a stance over the ball, swinging the club in the ways I suggest.

That is the purpose of the book. It was not put together merely to provide interesting, easy reading. It was prepared to instruct. Make it your golfing textbook. Pull it out and look through it every now and then. You will be surprised when you run across something about a sand shot, which I discuss in Chapter 6, that will solve a problem you have encountered with your bunker play at the club.

And practice. With the intended simplicity of these illustrated lessons, you will have little trouble understanding the instruction. But application comes only with plenty of practice.

Play away.

AN ORIGINAL PAPERBACK SERIES • Edited by Don Congdon

COMBAT: WORLD WAR I

The story of the "war to end all wars" as it has never been told before—eye-witness reports of the great battles fought on land, at sea, and for the first time in the air. Foreword and afterword by William Manchester. Introduction by Herbert Mitgang. **75c**

COMBAT: WORLD WAR II

EUROPEAN THEATER These authoritative first-hand accounts recreate in full dimension the historic battle for Europe, from an overview of grand strategy to the fox-hole view of the individual rifleman. Introduction by Merle Miller. **60c**

PACIFIC THEATER From the bombing of Pearl Harbor to the destruction of the Japanese fleet in Leyte Gulf, here is the war as recorded by the men who fought it. Introduction by Merle Miller. **60c**

THE WAR WITH JAPAN On-the-spot reports of the war with Japan—the ships, the planes, and the men who turned defeat into victory. Introduction by Richard Tregaskis. **60c**

THE WAR WITH GERMANY From Dunkirk to the fall of the Third Reich—the war with Germany recreated in all its fury by the men who fought it. Introduction by Herbert Mitgang. **60c**

Each volume complete with maps and running commentary.

DELL BOOKS

If you cannot obtain copies of these titles at your local newsstand, just send the price (plus 10c per copy for handling and postage) to Dell Books, Box 2291, Grand Central Post Office, New York, N.Y. 10017. No postage or handling charge is required on any order of five or more books.

*An explosive novel of how the U.S. Army
used its twelve worst criminals*

THE
DIRTY
DOZEN

E. M. Nathanson

★ *A Literary Guild Selection in hardcover*

★ *Now a major motion picture
starring Lee Marvin, Ernest Borgnine,
and Jimmy Brown*

The most original and savage novel of World
War II since *From Here to Eternity* . . .

"Tense action . . . gripping . . . highly recommended"
—*Book of the Month Club News*
"If you're in the mood for a marvelous thriller, read this one."
—*Cosmopolitan*

A DELL BOOK   95c

Don't Miss These
Bestsellers From Dell

THE SECRET OF SANTA VITTORIA Robert Crichton 95c

GAMES PEOPLE PLAY Eric Berne M.D. $1.25

THE FIXER Bernard Malamud 95c

THE DIRTY DOZEN E. M. Nathanson 95c

THE PAPER DRAGON Evan Hunter 95c

TAI-PAN James Clavell 95c

THERE IS A RIVER: THE STORY OF EDGAR CAYCE
Thomas Sugrue 95c

I, A WOMAN Siv Holm 75c

A DANDY IN ASPIC Derek Marlowe 75c

AN ODOR OF SANCTITY Frank Yerby 95c

THE DOCTORS Martin L. Gross $1.25

PEDLOCK & SONS Stephen Longstreet 95c

THE MENORAH MEN Lionel Davidson 75c

CAPABLE OF HONOR Allen Drury $1.25

BILLION DOLLAR BRAIN Len Deighton 75c

If you cannot obtain copies of these titles at your local bookseller's just send the price (plus 10c per copy for handling and postage) to Dell Books, Box 2291, Grand Central Post Office, New York, N.Y. 10017. No postage or handling charge is required on any order of five or more books.